Step in to Study Counselling

A Students' Guide to Learning Counselling and Tackling Course Assignments

2nd edition

Pete Sanders

PCCS BOOKS

Ross-on-Wye

First published in 1995
2nd edition published 1998

PCCS BOOKS
Llangarron
Ross-on-Wye
HR9 6PT
Tel (01989) 77 07 07
Fax (01989) 77 07 00

This selection © PCCS BOOKS
pp.100 & 101 © Rose Cameron, pp.90 & 91 © Alan Frankland, p.143 © Lynn Myint-Maung,
pp.86 & 87 © Janet Tolan, pp.41 - 43 © Tracey & Martyn Walshaw.

Step in to *Study* Counselling - A Students Guide to Learning Counselling and Tackling Course Assignments 2nd edition

ISBN 1 898059 19 5

Cover design by Peter Kneebone
Printed by Redwood Books, Trowbridge, Wiltshire.

Contents

Acknowledgements

I would like all readers to know that this book would have looked very different if the following people had not made their contributions: Rose Cameron, Alan Frankland, Lynn Myint-Maung, Janet Tolan, Tracey Walshaw and Martyn Walshaw. Also, to Barbara Cordwell, whose work appears unacknowledged in the text in order to keep the conventions I have chosen regarding the titling of boxes and panels.

There is also a short list of 'invisible' contributors whose work appears in highly abridged form as assignments and who will remain anonymous, partly in order to preserve confidences. Thanks to them too, they know who they are.

I would like to thank the British Association for Counselling, not only for permission to reprint the Code of Ethics and Practice for Trainers, but also the helpful and generous spirit in which it was given.

I am happy to acknowledge the help given to me by Maggie, my partner, who I would have liked to list as co-author since without her, this book would not have appeared at all. There is a fine line between editorship and authoring and I'm afraid that although I might be able to generate plenty of accessible prose, I also generate plenty of grammatical glitches. It is Maggie who does all the grammatical cleansing necessary and since a good proportion of this book is about how to do written assignments, Maggie has steered the whole project away from too much 'shooting-itself-in-the-foot'.

Finally, although I have thanked past students in previous books, it rarely seems as though I am able to capture the true indebtedness I feel to the course participants who have taught me most of what I know as a trainer. Over the years I am sure that I have learned as much from them as they have from me.

Pete Sanders
Ross-on-Wye
June 1998

Introduction
(Read this first)

1

Why a book on study skills for counselling courses?
One of the great strengths of counselling courses is that they are made up of a great mix of people from all walks of life, from different social and economic backgrounds and life experiences. Some have been blessed (or cursed) with a rigorous education and some have not. As we wish to celebrate and acknowledge this rich mixture we want to cater for all trainee counsellors or counselling skills users which will mean including in this book information that is not relevant to everyone. Many of you will also be mature students returning to study after a number of years and are terrified at the thought of writing an essay or sitting an exam. There are no magic formulae, but there are some things you can do to get the very best out of your course.

It has been suggested that much of the information in study skills books is patronising nonsense that everyone knows already. I strongly disagree. It is my view that tutors who are afraid of saying the 'simple' thing that they have discovered by accident, or the 'obvious' thing that they were told but have forgotten by whom, are the real culprits. It is patronising to *not* share the things we know, however simple they might be. It is my experience that many adult learners have been led to believe that studying is a mystery or somehow 'in your genes'. This is the real nonsense, and I make no apologies for stating what a lucky few think is the obvious.

Whilst reading this book (but not because of it I hope) some of you will lose heart and not put as much effort into studying: a few will drop out of their course altogether. This lack of motivation cannot be cured by study skills hints and tips but some writers have suggested ways of overcoming temporary spells in the doldrums when you are wondering whether it's all worthwhile. My favourite involves writing down ten (any number up to ten will do) reasons for doing this course and passing these assessments. Pin it up in a prominent position where you do your studying or put it in the inside cover of your folder. If you feel like giving up it will be there to remind you just what you're doing it all for!

Studying, writing essays and passing exams are *skills,* and like any other skills everyone can become reasonably good at them, though this requires application and practice. However, there is no panacea to solve everyone's problem; no single method or plan can suit all students.

Who is this book for?
This book is for anyone wanting to improve performance on counselling course assignments. That includes both types of course participant - trainees and tutors. As a tutor I seem to spend hours supporting and guiding trainees through assignments and have longed for a book that would help me do it better. To be more honest, I guess that what I'm after

is a book that will take the burden off me, as a tutor; so this book, then, is written to help me too!

What is in the book

The book is part information, part helpful (I hope) suggestion and part activity based awareness raising. It is *all* intended to be empowering. I cannot pretend that as a student or a tutor I have always followed my own good advice. More often than not I have had the good fortune to be able to learn by my own mistakes without hurting myself or others too much. The book is about what I, and others, have *aimed at*, and I know that successful study is founded on clear aims.

Human beings are particularly well equipped to acquire knowledge and skills and to solve problems. It is most unfortunate, therefore, that many students look upon academic work as an 'art' and the capacity to study as a 'gift'. It would be better to look upon studying as a skilled activity (rather like the way we look upon helping or counselling). Also, like counselling, it helps to develop self-awareness so that you can improve your weak points and play to your strengths. Successful studying is as much an attitude as it is a skill. It requires self-confidence built upon a keen appreciation of one's own abilities, plus a belief that improvement is possible.

Another feature of studying and learning as activities is that they are most often done with, or at the very least in the presence of, other people. (This particularly applies to the study of counselling.) So, like in counselling and helping, relationships are also important in learning. It always pays to remember that your fellow course participants are in a relationship with you, and that tutors are people too. If this could be written down as a formula it would go something like this:

Self-awareness
and learning through
Relationships
plus
Knowledge of good learning strategies
plus
Information about the nature of assessment
equals
Improvement in the skills of successful study

However important to your learning the tutors on your course might be, never forget that your fellow course participants bring with them a huge catalogue of experience. If you are open to it, you can learn *at least* as much from your peers as you can learn from your tutors. Your peers can help you learn not only about counselling, but also about studying itself. How do they work best? What have they found helpful? What was their essay like and why did they get different marks and comments from you? There is a mine of good experience and information about learning and studying both within yourself and in the seat next to you. When we look at **Learning Environments** in Chapter 3 you will see that it is largely within your power to get the best out of the situation and people in it - that includes yourself, your peers and your tutors.

Deja Vu

As you read through the book you may well get the 'I'm sure I've seen that before' feeling. The book is more repetitive than most because the same themes keep repeating themselves throughout learning and assessment processes. Hopefully there will be a slightly different slant each time.

Panels and Pages

You will find various types of panel and page scattered around the book to break up the monotonous tone:

Inside Stories

These are personal accounts of counselling training from the viewpoints of the main protagonists. The trainee, the tutor, the external examiner, the supervisor of trainee counsellors, the trainee's partner and family all have something to say about how their lives are touched by counselling training. These personal stories might be entertaining, but their real purpose is to be read in the spirit of Carl Rogers' famous assertion that *'what is most personal is most universal.'* These accounts may encourage you to share your own experiences with colleagues, fellow course participants, friends and family, or you could leave the book open at key pages for others to 'accidentally' see!

Activities

Throughout the book you will be invited to interact with the text by thinking in certain ways, answering questions, filling in gaps, or occasionally talking with peers or friends. These activities come in a number of different forms, but are not always set apart as activity panels. Sometimes they are embedded in the text. The general rule is that anything that can be read or done as a stand-alone activity is in a panel. If it requires the support of the surrounding text to give it sense and purpose, it will be embedded in the text.

Model Answers

These panels present completed work (or sections of completed work) together with tutor's comments. The idea is to give some insight into the process of writing and marking - both from the tutor's point of view (on a couple of occasions), but also so that *you* can try your hand at peer evaluation. It is not my intention to offer these as 'perfect' answers, since they quite clearly are not. Don't be tempted to copy them, other than getting an idea or two about the general method of tackling a particular assignment. They are based on real assignments done by real students, so read them respectfully. Where necessary names and sufficient factual detail have been changed to render any persons mentioned unrecognisable.

Hints and Tips

No book on study skills would be complete without some hints and tips. These are summaries of the major points *and* additional ideas collected in point form in panels at the end of each chapter.

Did you know...?

Is there any evidence to back up study techniques? Here we will see whether we can use any findings from psychology to help improve our studying.

All others (various panels)

How to read this book (This is important!)

On no account should anyone try to read this book from cover to cover. You will end up reading some things you know already and you will suffer *severely* from deja vu (see above). You might also feel terminally patronised (also see above). There is no *correct* way to read it as long as you don't read it from cover to cover. It's like a recipe book in some parts and so is repetitive - recipe books keep on saying 'fold in the ingredients with a metal spoon' etc., whereas I keep on saying 'plan your work'.

In order to prepare for your course or as general background reading you should read Chapters 1, 2, 3 and 5, then use the remainder as a cookbook to read as-and-when you need to. You can also, of course, dip in and read the *Inside Stories* whenever you like.

Standards, protection and complaints

We live in a consumer and customer-oriented culture. You are a consumer of counselling training and as such have rights and responsibilities. As a participant in a counselling training programme, your interests are looked after in a number of ways:

1. The responsibility you take for looking after your own interests. This book is an attempt to help you do this by explaining the whole area of course assessment and assignments.

2. The organisation which delivers your course - whether it is a college, university or privately run training institute - should have some internal and external systems in place for monitoring and improving standards and quality of provision. These should include having a complaints procedure, an external examiner or moderator and in some cases a course consultant. (All of these are recommended by the British Association for Counselling.) Courses are also encouraged to appoint an external complaints mediator - someone who arbitrates when complaints are made and is uninvolved with the course, so that they can take as objective a view as possible. (See *Your Rights as a Student - Training Contracts* on page 35.) In addition, you will be able to give feedback on your course (see BAC Code, pages 9-13, section B4.5) and the feedback should be considered and if appropriate acted upon by the course team.

3. The validating body - this might be a university, a college or a national or regional independent body. The validating body will have standards that it will monitor by appointing moderators or external examiners. They can also adjudicate in the case of disputes or complaints made by trainees. (See *Inside Story: The External Examiner* on pages 86 & 87.)

4. Finally the British Association for Counselling publish a Code of Ethics and Practice for Trainers. If your trainers or training organisation are members of BAC they will be bound by this, and the other BAC Codes of Ethics and Practice. This code is backed up by a complaints procedure. The code is reprinted in full on the following pages with the kind permission of BAC.

Your responsibilities

If you ask that high standards are maintained by your trainers, they can expect high standards from you in return. Getting the most from your training means that:

Firstly, you are fully committed and motivated, i.e. you are not doing it 'just for the piece of paper'.

Secondly, you get fully involved, not sitting at the

edge, unwilling to contribute. Counselling training *requires* involvement and participation. Involvement in not optional.

Thirdly, you are prepared to bring as much of your whole, your real self as you can, risky and scary though this will undoubtedly be at times.

Fourthly, abide by the organisations rules, i.e. do not act in an aggressive, racist, sexist, abusive or offensive way.

Finally, if things are not going well, talk to tutors first and as soon as possible. Explore all informal methods of resolving problems before you make a formal complaint. Make positive suggestions - even if you're not asked to - and fill in course evaluation sheets honestly.

At various stages of counselling training, your responsibilities might go even further than this. When you wish to carry your training to a professional level, i.e. you are on a diploma-level course training to be a counsellor, you will have responsibilities to your clients. You will attend to this by being in supervision whilst you are practising as a trainee and beyond into your career as a counsellor.

You might wish to further protect your clients by taking out insurance to cover your practice. The British Association for Counselling can give information and advice on this. In addition I would urge all readers to look at what Dave Mearns has to say on the topic in *Questions and Answers on Counselling in Action*, edited by Windy Dryden.

Choosing the right course for you
You and Your Needs
• Do you know what counselling approach or model

you want to learn? There are many different approaches. If you are unclear, you should ask for clarification or attend an introductory course or do some voluntary work to find out more about the basics of helping using counselling skills. Do you want to train to be a person-centred counsellor, an integrative, psychodynamic, cognitive behavioural, TA or Gestalt counsellor?

• What pattern of attendance would best suit you, your lifestyle and your learning needs. Some full-time one year courses are offered, but the vast majority of training is offered as part-time courses run over two, three or more years. Some one-year courses are very intensive. The work load is huge and you may not have time to fit it all in.

• Fees for counselling training can be considerable. Some institutions offer reduced fees for unemployed or disabled students. You may have to seek a course that you can afford. It is not always the case that the most expensive course is the best.

The College or Training Provider, Staff and Resources
• Shop around - apply to many places within reasonable travelling distance. Compare validation (BAC, UKCP, Centra, Open College, etc.) fees and staff qualifications.

• Visit the premises, have a look around, compare facilities.

• Are the staff fully qualified - do they all have professional diplomas in counselling? How many have teaching or training qualifications? How experienced are they, as counsellors, as trainers and as supervisors? (They should have at least couple of years experience as a qualified counsellor, and the more experience as a trainer the better.) Are they supervised? Are they *BAC Accredited Counsellors*? Are they *BAC Accredited Trainers*? (BAC Accredited Counsellors and Accredited Trainers have demonstrated that they have appropriate qualifications and *supervised* experience and that they are committed to continuing professional development, i.e. they go on courses regularly.)

• Have the staff received *specific* training in the core theoretical approach taught on the course? This is particularly relevant for Person-Centred Courses, since some people think that *anyone* can be a person-centred trainer. What qualifications do the staff have? If the course is integrative or eclectic does the staff team have a broad range of qualifications and experience?

• Make sure the staff are individual members of a professional body such as BAC or UKCP and that the college or institute is an organisational member of such a body. Trainers and organisations that belong to such bodies are bound by codes of ethics and practice.

• Are the training rooms comfortable and quiet? Is there enough (any?) audio and video equipment to go around? (Regular use of video equipment is one of the best ways of developing counselling skills.)

• Does the college or institute employ an external examiner, an external course consultant and an external complaints mediator? (All three are recommended by BAC and should be different people, experienced and independent.)

The Course.

• Is it validated by a reputable independent external body, e.g. University, Open College, Centra?

• Is it accredited by a professional body such as BAC, or does it meet the accreditation requirements? Contact BAC for an up-to-date list of Accredited courses in your area.

• Is there a balance on the course between skills, practice experience (and supervision), theory and personal development? Do the tutors explain how this fits together on the course?

• Is there a '*Core Theoretical Model*' or main theory underpinning the course? Some courses are *Integrative* and have a single integrative model (such as Egan or Lazarus) as their model. Beware of courses that just offer a mish mash of approaches without giving you enough time to learn properly and become skilled at any.

• The course publicity (or tutors) should clearly explain what counselling approach is used on the course. Staff should ideally belong to some appropriate organisation (such as the International Transactional Analysis Association, or the British Association for the Person Centred Approach) according to the approach being taught. Beware of courses that seem unclear about this.

• The course philosophy should be in harmony with the core theoretical model. A course that claimed to be person-centred, for example should embody the central tenets and attitudes of person-centred learning. It should be student-led, with plenty of student self and peer assessment. Person-centred theory should be to the fore and there should not be too much theory from other approaches.

• How many hours training does the course offer? Some courses count break times as training (this is not acceptable to bodies such as BAC). Courses should provide sufficient hours to add up to at least 450 hours for BAC Individual Accreditation purposes. Any less than this and you will not be able to apply for Accreditation when you have completed your practice hours without doing further training. If in any doubt phone BAC for clarification.

General

- What is the *total* cost of the training? You will need to add the cost of some further books, tapes stationary etc. Some fees are not inclusive - you may have to pay extra for, e.g. supervision, or even residentials. These extra costs can come to hundreds of pounds.
- How long is the course - will your employer give you study leave for the required time period?
- If it's a Diploma or professional level course, does it require an appropriate level of supervision for your client practice? Are you expected to find your own supervisor? How do you know whether they are experienced enough or follow the same core model as your training? Who will pay?
- Are there reduced cost places for unwaged applicants? Can you pay by instalments?
- Is there an Equal Opportunities Statement or Policy, is there a Complaints Procedure? Can you see them?
- Can you meet past and present students in the absence of course staff to get the *truth* about what the course is really like? (BAC recommend that applicants should be able to do this.)

If in any doubt about what is good practice, contact BAC (address on p.160). The BAC produces leaflets summarising their recommendations and a Training Directory with guidance for applicants. All reputable counselling training providers should be organisational members of BAC and should have copies of the leaflets and the Training Directory. If a course chooses to not adhere to BAC recommended good practice, they should be able to explain why - **there *are* some good, defensible reasons for opting out** and the course team should be able to demonstrate a principled stance.

The British Association for Counselling

As a student of counselling, you could look to the BAC as more than a remote organisation providing services only for professional counsellors. I would strongly recommend all trainees on diploma-level professional courses to join BAC (or the equivalent professional body in the country where you live.). It looks after the interests of students in a number of ways, as can be seen immediately by the Code reprinted on the next few pages. The BAC also publish directories and booklets giving information on where to find and how to choose your counselling training. For some of you it may seem that this information is coming a little late in the day, since you may already be committed to a particular training course or pathway.

If you are in training to become a professional counsellor, your ultimate aim may be entry in the UK Register of Counsellors. In order to do this, you will have to become an Accredited Counsellor. The first way in which the BAC can help you is for you to discover whether the training pathway or course you are following will meet the qualification requirements for individual counsellor accreditation. The BAC quarterly journal *Counselling* is a good mix of current affairs, academic discourse and a forum for debate about contemporary issues in counselling and therapy, in short the BAC is a meeting-place and talking shop for those interested in counselling. That should include you! You can find the address on page 160.

The 'Profession' of Counselling - antidotes and alternatives

In recent years a difference in view has arisen between groups of practitioners about whether counselling and psychotherapy should become a 'profession'. Even amongst those who are generally in favour of the professionalisation of counselling, there is anxiety about the nature of the profession.

It is easy for people entering into training to miss this whole debate since courses have hitherto paid little or no attention to the whole issue. It is impossible to try a summary here of the complex issues involved, but I think it is important that trainees go into training knowing that there is a growing number of counsellors and therapists who have grave doubts about the increasing professionalisation of this work. This growing number includes many extremely well-known writers, theorists, practitioners and trainers, so don't get suckered by anyone who suggests that it is a small 'lunatic fringe'.

I have been criticised myself (Tudor 1997) for not giving enough prominence to alternatives to the BAC and UKCP and I fear that even this half-page will not satisfy many people. The best way to acquaint yourself with the issues is to read about it. The main problem is that this debate has no natural large stage. By this I mean that BAC, for example, itself committed to creating a profession of counselling, can hardly be blamed for not promoting arguments that run against the project of creating a profession. The difficulties do not end there. Richard Mowbray wrote a highly contentious book *The Case Against Psychotherapy Registration: A Conservation Issue for the Human Potential Movement* and had to publish it himself since no publisher would touch it. More recently the debate has found a wider audience through *Implausible Professions: Arguments for Pluralism and Autonomy in Counselling and Psychotherapy* edited by Richard House and Nick Totton, and the British Psychological Society Division of Counselling Psychology invited Nick Totton to speak at their Annual Conference. These two books should be essential reading for all counselling trainees.

Trainees should also be aware of the emergence of a real alternative to professional bodies such as BAC, BPS and UKCP, namely the Independent Practitioners Network (IPN), address on p.160. The following are extracts from the IPN Interim Constitution:

1. The Network exists to further and support among its members good practice which is open about its aims and underlying principles.
2. The Network also seeks to provide people looking for help with a context of basic security within which to make their own decisions about which practitioner and which form of work is appropriate for them, in the confidence that Network members are able to provide and sustain a suitable environment for the work they offer.
3. To the above ends, member groups recognise that practitioners must take responsibility for ensuring that they are able adequately to fulfil their role. Member groups are committed to supporting this responsibility through continuous self and peer assessment, monitoring and challenge.
5. The Network has no commitment to any specific model of therapy, therapeutic training or the therapeutic relationship. It specifically favours diversity and ecological complexity.

British Association for Counselling
Code of Ethics and Practice for Trainers

1. The Status of this Code
1.1 In response to the experience of members of BAC this Code is a revision of the 1996 Code

Structure of this Code
A. A Code of Ethics for all Trainers.
B. A general Code of Practice for all Trainers
C. Additional clause for Trainers in Counselling.
D. Additional clauses for Trainers in Counselling Skills

2. Introduction
2.1 The purpose of this Code of Ethics and Practice is to establish and maintain standards for trainers who are members of BAC and to inform and protect members of the public seeking training in counselling, counselling skills or counselling-related areas, whatever the level or length of the training programme. Training in counselling-related areas includes training in counselling supervision, group work, interpersonal skills and other topics involving counselling theory and practice.

Sections A and B apply to all trainers. Section C contains an additional clause for trainers in counselling. Section D contains additional clauses for trainers in counselling skills.

2.2 The document must be seen in relation to all other BAC Codes of Ethics and Practice and BAC Course Recognition Procedures.
2.3 There is an important relationship between the agency employing the trainer and the trainee undertaking the training. This Code reinforces the principle that agencies which are organisational members of BAC abide by all BAC codes.
2.4 Ethical standards comprise such values as integrity, impartiality and respect. Anti-discriminatory practice reflects the basic values of counselling and training.

Members of BAC, in assenting to this Code, accept their appropriate responsibilities as trainers, to trainees, trainees' clients, employing agencies, colleagues, this Association and to the wider community.
2.5 In the context of this Code, trainers are those who train people in counselling, in counselling skills or in counselling-related areas. They should be experienced and competent practitioners. Trainers have a responsibility to draw the attention of trainees to all BAG Codes of' Ethics and Practice.
2.6 Trainers must be aware that there are differences between training in counselling training in counselling skills and training in counselling-related areas. Trainees must be made aware of this and trainers should endeavour to ensure that their intending trainees join an appropriate training programme.
2.7 There should be consistency between the theoretical orientation of the programme and the training methods and, where they are used, methods of assessment and evaluation (e.g. client-centred courses would normally be trainee-centred).
2.8 Training is at its most effective when there are two or more trainers. Trainers and their employing agencies have a responsibility to ensure this wherever possible.
2.9 The size of the group must be congruent with the training objectives and the model of working. Decisions about staff:student ratios must take account of the learning objectives and methods of assessment and of the importance of being able to give individual attention and recognition to each course member. Where direct feedback between trainer and trainee is an important part of the course a maximum staff to student ratio of 1:12 is recommended best practice.

A Code of Ethics for All Trainers
A.1 Values
Training is a non-exploitative activity. Its basic values are integrity, impartiality and respect. Trainers must take the same degree of care to work ethically whether the training is paid or unpaid.

British Association for Counselling
Code of Ethics and Practice for Trainers...
continued

A.2 Anti-discrimination
Trainers must consider and address their own prejudices and stereotyping. They must also address the prejudices and stereotyping of their trainees. They must ensure that an anti-discriminatory approach is integral to all the training they provide.

A.3 Safety
All reasonable steps shall be taken by trainers to ensure the safety of trainees and clients during training.

A.4 Competence
Trainers must take all reasonable steps to monitor and develop their competence as trainers and work within the limits of that competence.

A.5 Confidentiality
Trainers must clarify the limits of confidentiality within the training process at the beginning of the training programme.

A.6 Contracts
The terms and conditions on which the training is offered must be made clear to trainees before the start of the training programme. Subsequent revision of these terms must be agreed in advance of any changes.

A.7 Boundaries
Trainers must maintain and establish appropriate boundaries between themselves and their trainees so that working relationships are not confused with friendship or other relationships.

B.   *General Code of Practice for all Trainers*
B. 1 Responsibility

B.1.1 Trainers deliberately undertake the task of delivering training in counselling, counselling skills and counselling-related areas.

B.1.2 Trainers are responsible for observing the principles embodied in this Code of Ethics and Practice and all current BAC Codes and for introducing trainees to the BAC Codes of Ethics and Practice in the early stages of the training programme.

B.1.3 Trainers must recognise the value and dignity of trainees, with due regard to issues of origin, status, gender, age, beliefs, sexual preference or disability. Trainers have a responsibility to be aware of, and address their own issues of prejudice and stereotyping, and to give particular consideration to ways in which this may impact on the training.

B.1.4 Trainers have a responsibility to encourage and facilitate the self-development and self-awareness of trainees, so that trainees learn to integrate practice and personal insights.

B.1.5 Trainers are responsible for making explicit to trainees the boundaries between training, counselling supervision, consultancy, counselling and the use of counselling skills.

B.1.6 Trainers are responsible for modelling appropriate boundaries.

1.6.1 The roles of trainee and client must be kept separate during the training; where painful personal issues are revealed, trainers are responsible for suggesting and encouraging further in-depth work with a counsellor outside the training context.

1.6.2 The providers of counselling for trainees during the programme must be independent of the training context and any assessment procedures.

1.6.3 Trainers should take all reasonable steps to ensure that any personal and social contacts between them and their trainees do not adversely influence the effectiveness of the training.

British Association for Counselling
Code of Ethics and Practice for Trainers...
continued

B.1.7 Trainers must not accept current clients as trainees. Former trainees must not become clients, nor former clients become trainees, until a period of time has elapsed for reflection and after consultation with a counselling supervisor.

B.1.8 Trainers are responsible for ensuring that their emotional needs are met outside the training work and are not dependent on their relationships with trainees.

B.1.9 Trainers must not exploit their trainees financially, sexually, emotionally, or in any other way. Engaging in sexual activity with trainees is unethical.

B.1.10 Trainers must ensure that consideration is given to the appropriateness of the settings in which trainees propose to, or are expected to, work on completion of the training programme.

B.1.11 Trainers are expected, when appropriate, to prepare trainees to practice effectively within their work setting.

B.1.12 Trainers have a responsibility to ensure that appropriate counselling supervision arrangements are in place for trainees where working with clients is part of the course.

B.1.13 Visiting or occasional trainers on programmes must ensure that they take responsibility for any former or current pre-existing professional or personal relationship with any member of the training group.

B.1.14 Trainers must acknowledge the individual life experience and identity of trainees Challenges to the views, attitudes and outlooks of trainees must be respectful, related to the stated objectives of the course, and model good practice.

B.1.15 Trainers are responsible for discussing with trainees any needs for personal counselling and the contribution it might make to the trainees' work both during and after the programme.

B.1.16 Trainers must at all times conduct themselves in their training activities in ways which will not undermine public confidence in their role as trainers, in the work of other trainers or in the role of BAC.

B.2. Competence

B.2.1 It is strongly recommended that trainers should have completed at least one year's post-training experience as practitioners in an appropriate field of work. They should commit themselves to continuing professional development as trainers.

B.2.2 Trainers must monitor their training work and be able and willing to account to trainees and colleagues for what they do and why.

B.2.3 Trainers must monitor and evaluate the limits of their competence as trainers by means of regular supervision or consultancy.

B.2.4 Trainers have a responsibility to themselves and to their trainees to maintain their own effectiveness, resilience and ability to work with trainees. They are expected to monitor their own personal functioning and to seek help and/or agree to withdraw from training, whether temporarily or permanently, when their personal resources are so depleted as to require this.

B.3 Confidentiality

B.3.1 Trainers are responsible for establishing a contract for confidential working which makes explicit the responsibilities of both trainer and trainees.

B.3.2 Trainers must inform trainees at the beginning of the training programme of all reasonably foreseeable circumstances under which confidentiality may be breached during the training programme.

B.3.3 Trainers must not reveal confidential information concerning trainees, or former trainees, without the permission of the trainee, except:

   a. in discussion with those on whom trainers rely for professional support and supervision. (These discussions will usually be anonymous and the supervisor is bound by confidentiality)

British Association for Counselling
Code of Ethics and Practice for Trainers...
continued

b. in order to prevent serious harm to another or to the trainee

c. when legally required to break confidentiality;

d. during selection, assessment, complaints and disciplinary procedures in order to prevent or investigate breaches of ethical standards by trainees.

If consent to the disclosure of confidential information has been withheld, trainees should normally be informed in advance that a trainer intends to disclose confidential information.

B.3.4 Detailed information about specific trainees, or former trainees, may be used for publication or in meetings only with the trainees' permission and with anonymity preserved. Where trainers need to use examples from previous work to illustrate a point to trainees, this must be done respectfully, briefly and anonymously.

B.3.5 If discussion by trainers of their trainees, or former trainees, with professional colleagues becomes necessary, it must be purposeful, not trivialising, and relevant to the training.

B.3.6 If trainers suspect misconduct by another trainer which cannot be resolved or remedied after discussion with the trainer concerned, they should implement any internal complaints procedures that may be available or the BAC Complaints Procedure. Any required breaches of confidentiality should be limited to those necessary for the investigation of the complaint.

B.4 Management of the Training Work

B.4.1 Trainers must make basic information available to potential trainees, in writing or by other appropriate means of communication, before the start of the programme. This should include:

a. the fees to be charged and any other expenses which may be incurred;

b. the dates and time commitments;

c. information on selection procedures, entry requirements and the process by which decisions are made;

d. basic information about the content of the programme, its philosophical and theoretical approach and the training methods to be used;

e. the relevant qualifications of the trainers;

f. any requirements for counselling supervision or personal counselling which trainees will be expected to comply with while training;

g. guidelines for work experience or placements to be undertaken as part of the training

h. evaluation and assessment methods to be used during the programme and the implications of these;

i. if the programme carries a qualification, arrangements for appeals should a dispute arise.

B.4.2 Trainers must check whether training is being undertaken voluntarily or compulsorily and, if necessary, draw employers' attention to the fact that a voluntary commitment is the more appropriate.

B.4.3 Trainers should ensure that trainees receive regular feedback on their work and that self and peer assessment are encouraged at regular intervals.

B.4.4 Trainers must be alert to any prejudices and assumptions that trainees reveal and raise their awareness of these issues, so that trainees are encouraged to recognise and value difference,

B.4.5 Trainers should ensure that trainees are given the opportunity to discuss their experiences of the programme and are also invited to evaluate these individually, in groups, or both, at least once in a training programme.

B.4.6 Trainers who become aware of a conflict between their obligation to a trainee and their obligation to an agency or organisation employing them, must make explicit to both the trainee and the agency or organisation employing them the nature and existence of this conflict

British Association for Counselling
Code of Ethics and Practice for Trainers...
continued

and seek to resolve it.

B.4.7 Where differences between trainer and trainee, or between trainers, cannot be resolved the trainer and, where appropriate the trainer's line manager, should consult with, and when necessary refer to, an independent expert.

C. Additional Clause for Trainers in Counselling

C.1 Trainers are encouraged to ensure that:

    a. practical experience as a counsellor in an external setting is, where possible, part of the training programme.

    b. the setting where trainees propose to practice as counsellors is appropriate, paying particular attention to the need for confidentiality, privacy and counselling supervision.

D Additional Clauses for Trainers in Counselling Skills

D.1 Trainers are responsible for ensuring that their trainees consider the appropriateness of the setting in which they use their counselling skills.

D.2 Trainers should ensure that trainees are clear that using counselling skills may lead to conflicting responsibilities. These should be discussed on the training course and in supervision.

Effective from 1 January 1997

Hints and Tips 1

1. Become and active participant in learning, not a passive onlooker. A counselling course is something *you do*, not something that *happens to you.*

2. Prepare for your course - collect all the relevant documents together and read them. It will make the first day less stressful if you don't have to ask so many questions.
   • Make a list of the things you do want to know.
   • Expect some things to have changed - all courses 'develop' due to the changing educational environment, government requirements and general improvements.

3. If you have a book list, read any books that have been recommended to you as sound preparation for the course.

4. If you are preparing for a diploma course, seriously consider joining the British Association for Counselling, or the equivalent professional body in the country where you live.

5. Read the BAC Code of Ethics and Practice for Trainers in Counselling and Counselling Skills. It tells you what to expect in the way of good practice in training.

6. Skim through this book to see what the chapter titles mean in reality. Look at the list of contents and make a note of the bits you want to read first.

7. Make a list of your strengths and weaknesses as a student, based on your past experience.
   • Read the relevant parts of this book to help with your weaknesses.
   • Make sure you acknowledge your strengths and play to them.

8. Do try my suggestion of writing as many reasons for doing the course as you can. Keep this in front of you for those 'low patches'. You might be able to amend it or add to it as you go through the course.

9. When it comes to choosing the right course for you remember to check:
   • the theoretical orientation of the course;
   • the training methods used on the course;
   • who validated the course - independent organisation, professional body or the college itself;
   • the tutors qualifications;
   • the accommodation, equipment and facilities;
   • whether the contact hours will be sufficient for your requirements.

Learning processes on counselling courses

2

There are three types or ways of learning which predominate on counselling courses and lead some students to think that the experience is *very* different from learning, say, GCSE Maths. (Educationalists would argue, however, that all types of learning come in to play in all subjects, and others would argue that all learning is experiential.) These three types of learning are:

- Experiential learning
- Learning in groups
- Personal or self-development

Experiential learning

Although we might think that the term simply means 'learning through experience', experiential learning has many different meanings. We will look at a few here which have special relevance to counselling. The term is probably most frequently associated with the *experiential learning cycle* described most fully by Kolb in 1984.

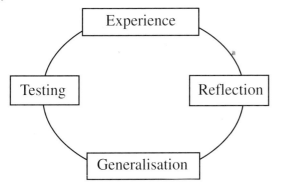

This general and rather abstract model has been used to help us understand how best to arrange learning experiences for, particularly adult, students. There have been many attempts to add to the ideas or tailor them to specific learning situations, but I include it here so that you can think about *you* as a learner and how you learn best.

Experience
Experiential learning requires personal and practical involvement in the thing being learned. That is to say that it is *learning by doing* rather than learning by merely *knowing*. This admirably suits the experiential learning model to counselling. So the first stage of experiential learning is to have an experience of some kind, maybe an activity or structured exercise or the experience of being a client or counsellor. This then provides fuel for the next stage of the learning cycle.

Reflection
It is important to provide opportunities for personal reflection on the experience - even if you simply ask yourself *'What the hell happened there?'*. Sometimes this is helped by sharing your experiences in groups.

Generalisation
This is our attempt to apply what is learned in one rather narrow setting (e.g. in a five minute exercise on a counselling course) to a wider set of contexts (e.g. practice as a counsellor in a variety of settings).

Testing

Finally we try out our new learning - sometimes in real life - and that provides us with a new experience, so we start the cycle all over again. Experiential learning becomes a permanent state of learning and development.

So we can see how the experiential learning cycle takes us from narrow course based experiences through to real life settings, but you would be wrong to think that learning games, exercises and role-plays are the only ways of learning experientially on counselling courses.

There are many types of activities which might be involved in the experiential learning of counselling. Within each of these sub-headings we could write out a list of possible activities that students and tutors might together negotiate as valuable contributions to counselling training, for example:
   • *Prior learning and prior experience:*
Assembling a portfolio of qualifications and experience, assessing competencies.
   • *Personal development and/or personal therapy:*
Group and individual therapy, creative/expressive approaches, visualisation, setting personal learning goals, keeping diaries and journals.
   • *Autonomous learning:*
Setting personal learning goals, negotiating learning contracts, challenging power dynamics of learning relationships.
   • *Client work or work placement:*
Setting up your own client sessions or work placement, professional relationships with other helpers on work placement, supervision/

mentorship.
   • *Problem solving in class and in the real-world:*
Exercises, brainstorming, generating, testing and evaluating action plans.
   • *Project work/research:*
Surveys, experiments, case studies, field work, interviews, presentation of results.
   • *Awareness-development exercises:*
Simulations, role-plays, games.
   • *One-to-one skills practice sessions with peers:*
Listening, giving and receiving feedback, providing and receiving core conditions.
   • *Community meetings and other learning groups involving interaction:*
Group discussion - listening and speaking in groups, evaluation, giving and receiving feedback, challenge.
   • *Presentations of student work and student-led workshops or seminars:*
Presenting ideas and experience, demonstrations, feedback from group sessions, videos and tapes of client work.

There are many opportunities for experiential learning in counselling training, and the list above is not exhaustive, it is just for illustration. You may well be able to add some new categories or activities of your own, or you might discover some different ways of learning through experience presented by tutors on your course. The above list might give you some ideas about new ways of learning.

Chapter 3 is intended to help you understand how to make the best use of the experiential learning methods available on your course, including becoming an autonomous learner. This is similar to the personal empowerment which, as counsellors, we aim to engender in our clients.

Learning in groups

You will spend the majority of the time on your course learning in groups. You may think that this is a fairly ordinary way of learning, since we have all experienced sitting in a classroom or lecture theatre with many other people when we were at school or college. There is, however, a big difference between learning in the presence of others (with little or no sense of connectedness other than being in the same room) and learning with, through and in relationship with others, where the connection between people is both the medium for, and the content of, the learning. Learning in groups on counselling courses is more often of the latter type, involving listening, speaking, sharing ideas and personal experiences and self-disclosure, rather than simple *group discussion.*

Perhaps I should have called this section 'collective learning', since the learning takes place through collective activities. There is a wide range of collective activities that we can engage in and it would be fair to say that, generally speaking, most of us are unused to working, living or even making simple decisions in this way. Inexperienced in collective living as we are, we will almost undoubtedly experience confusion, disorientation, and a whole host of other feelings from anger through sadness and boredom to exhilaration as we explore these new processes.

Sharing in groups

Being a member of any group is a social process that presents each of us with many challenges. When we are expected to learn from this process as well, it can sometimes feel too challenging. There are many tensions in group membership - to speak or not to speak, how much to say, what to say and when, how much to listen, how much to show of ourselves, and so on. The list is almost endless. One thing is true about groups, however, and that is that the majority of the people present are having to wrestle with much the same tensions as you. The other participants are likely to be just as worried about what is happening for them as they are about what you are saying.

The main activity in counselling course groups is sharing, rather than debate. Sharing is offering our thoughts, feelings and experiences, not to argue a point so much as cast light in the darkness or make and strengthen connections between group members. We can learn from the views and lives of others if we listen openly and without judgement. Sometimes another group member might say something that stirs strong feelings in us, from great sadness or anger to joy. Then we need to be honest and open in our responses (as opposed to our listening), so that we are genuine and not pretending to feel, for example, comfortable, when we are not.

So, sharing in groups can have several beneficial learning outcomes, for example:

• Sharing our thoughts in groups helps us solve problems and get new perspectives on issues. This 'many heads are better than one' effect is most noticeable when contributing views and experiences in order to make sense of a difficult theoretical point.

• It can help us 'ground' our ideas or make them concrete rather than abstract in our own or other people's experience.

• When in the presence of others, sometimes our thoughts and feelings seem to 'free up' and we think and feel more expansively.

• Ideas have a better chance of 'evolving' or developing when many contributions are made rather than getting stuck in a rut when we are on our own.

• We can gain support for our position or feel less isolated in our lives if other people describe similar feelings and experiences to the ones we have. We feel less of an 'island'.

• Notwithstanding the support we might get on particular life experiences or crises, being in a group is often experienced as *generally* supportive, i.e. it helps us keep up our morale when the daily or weekly grind of the course gets us down.

• We can practice the skills of counselling in groups by listening without judgement and being honest and genuine - trying to understand what someone is really saying.

• Group dynamics is best experienced and understood in groups rather than as a dry academic subject. This is another good example of experiential learning.

In order to oil the wheels of learning or facilitate the group process, tutors and student group members might develop particular ways of being in the group such as having rules about 'owning' feelings, thoughts and attitudes, rather than generalising. (This can mean simply remembering to say 'I am offended by what you said' or 'I have been wasting my time' rather than the blaming and generalising, 'That was an offensive thing to say' or 'We have totally wasted our time'.) Another way of facilitating the group learning process is to make sure that everyone who wants to, has the opportunity to speak, rather than it being 'survival of the loudest'.

Feeling safe in groups
Making simple rules about how a group conducts itself is sometimes called setting groundrules or making a group contract. These are covered in Chapter 3. In addition to rule making, there are several aspects of the physical setting which help us feel safe and these are also covered in Chapter 3.

Being silent in groups
Many of us have difficulty in contributing to group activity, and there can be many reasons for this. Most of the reasons originate within us, it is very rare that we can truly say that there simply wasn't time to have our say.

The trouble with this sort of difficulty is that the learning process in groups does require many varied contributions in order to work effectively. At a very basic level, some people *are* simply more talkative than others. Even when everyone in a group is relaxed, we might not make absolutely equal contributions to a group discussion, but again this doesn't explain why some of us hardly ever speak at all. The following points are worth considering about being consistently silent in a group. What do you think about these points and how do you feel about 'silent' group members? (Your opinions are likely to be influenced by how comfortable and confident you feel yourself about group membership and speaking in groups.)

• Some people are afraid to talk because they think that they have nothing sensible to say.

• It is difficult to say something if everyone else sounds more clever and articulate than you.

• Some people are crippled by embarrassment and completely 'dry up' at the prospect of speaking in a group.

• If you haven't got something sensible to say, it's best not to say anything.

• Everyone's contribution is helpful and of value, regardless of what it is.

• I don't find it easy to speak in groups and if I can take the risk and do it, then everyone should.

• I get just as much out of being silent as I do from talking. Groups need people to listen, just as much as they need people to talk.

• If I have a problem speaking in groups I should, as a trainee counsellor, address it and work on it, not just accept it and say 'It's just the way I am, I can't change.' Counselling and learning about counselling is about change, after all, and I should be 'up for it'.

• Everyone should say something because it shares the responsibility of doing the work of learning and it shows that we are committed and active, not just passengers along for the ride.

This last point is often raised in groups, namely, just how can we show appropriate commitment to learning in groups. Is it acceptable to remain silent and simply benefit from the efforts of others or should we not judge group members who prefer not to speak? It can be a source of frustration and anger to the active group members if they do not feel the work load has been shared out, and equally a source of frustration and anger to be judged by others in the group for remaining silent.

Enjoying group learning

If a substantial amount of time is going to be spent in groups and a substantial amount of the learning requires participation in groups, it will be torture if you find it unpleasant. It is sensible to work towards a position where it is at least bearable, if not actually enjoyable.

After considering the points in the last section, you might wonder whether it's worth the hassle, or you may be excited by the prospect of your next group session. I offer the following points to help tip the balance in favour of learning in groups since if you are on a counselling training course, you will undoubtedly be doing lots of it.

• Groups are not deliberately set up by tutors to be an ordeal. They are used because it is believed to be the best way of learning counselling.

• You have every right to your point of view and you have the right to express it.

• Try not to feel intimidated by others' apparent ease when speaking in groups.

• It often helps to say how you're feeling - i.e., that you're nervous about public speaking or that you don't know what to say.

• Don't wait until you have some blockbusting insight, or some brilliant point to make. You will wait forever. Group discussions move very quickly and by the time you have organised your words to express this wonderful idea, the emphasis will have shifted and moved on. It will seem as though there is *never* a *right* time to speak.

The Personal Development Group in Counselling Training

You will have noticed that we have included a Personal Development, or 'PD' Group on the course timetable and you may be wondering exactly what one is and what happens. The PD group consists of the student group meeting weekly for one and a half hours with a facilitator. This handout is intended to go a little way to explaining what a PD group is, although it is impossible to say what will happen in *your* PD group from week to week - that will be up to you.

The personal development group is an important part of counselling training. The aim is to provide a 'live' setting in which we can learn about ourselves in relationship with other people, by being in relationships with other people. It also helps us experience some of the feelings of being a client or at least engaging with our own process of self-directed change.

We have particularly chosen groups as a vehicle for personal development for a number of reasons:
• Groups provide a more varied social setting in which you will meet a wider range of people than in personal therapy, and you will, by the very nature of the group, be 'forced' into a relationship with them at least as group members.
• Groups can generate a strong sense of belonging, community and acceptance. This can provide an atmosphere which supports personal growth.
• Groups are powerful change agents in themselves, where members are able to experience strong feelings, both positive and negative, towards themselves and other group members.
• Groups give us the opportunity to observe others and share their experiences. Everyone has the opportunity to experiment with different degrees of self-disclosure, giving us insight into our attitudes, prejudices and behaviour patterns.

The facilitator is a trained and supervised counsellor and trainer whose job it is to help the group:
    • develop and maintain appropriate boundaries,
    • continue to focus on what is happening in the group,
    • provide a balance between support and challenge for group members.
It is up to each group member to share in the responsibility for what happens in the group.

Members of PD groups each discover something different about themselves, their relationships with others and working in groups. There are some common experiences, however, such as not knowing what is expected of you, feeling anxious when taking risks around self-disclosure and worrying about expressing yourself clumsily. Common themes in PD groups include group cohesion, inclusion and exclusion, affection, who is in control, trust, openness, conformity and cooperation. A powerful mixture of human issues and the central focus for counselling training. Being a member of your PD group will not always be comfortable, and there will always be much to learn.

• It is better to engage in the discussion in a more natural way. Don't be so ambitious, make some lower-key points and you will begin to feel relaxed. This is the way group learning happens, in small steps that everyone can follow and feel part of rather than a few brilliant points which leave most participants behind.

• Don't be afraid to ask questions of the tutor or other group members. It may be that you haven't followed the discussion, so ask for clarification or an example to help you understand. (It may well be the case that others don't understand either.)

• Keep it simple and straightforward whenever possible. And paradoxically, if you can't organise your thoughts and feelings into a simple coherent statement, don't worry, 'getting it out', even in a jumble, can help.

Personal or self-development

Known colloquially as PD and subject of many fables, horror stories and myths, personal development (frequently in groups) is a feature, some would say the central focus of, the vast majority of counselling training. There are some slight differences in the meaning of the term depending upon a number of factors including the theoretical approach of the course. These differences can lead to the personal development requirement of training being met in different ways.

Personal therapy, 'home' groups, PD and community groups are all personal development opportunities provided, strongly recommended or required by courses. Some courses use more than one of these methods at the same time. There are many different views on PD, the need for it and how it is best achieved. How does *your* course meet the PD requirement and what is the rationale behind it? If it is not made clear in the course documentation, ask one of the tutors to explain the reasoning behind the course PD provision.

A frequent experience on counselling courses is that the PD component is *never explained* to students. You may be left to find out for yourself and this can often feel like a struggle, especially when tutors seem perversely to withhold information as though there is some great 'truth' to discover. (This way of working has its origins in t-group and sensitivity training work pioneered by Kurt Lewin in the 1940s.)

Not all courses are like this, some do give information to facilitate the personal development process. An example of one such course handout is included on the page opposite (an extract, not the whole handout). You might find it helpful, but beware of becoming a 'groupie'. That is getting smart about what happens in groups and thinking to yourself (or even worse, *saying*) 'I know what is happening here - the group is at the 'storming' stage'. Learning in groups is an experience which must be had in its unfettered fullness and immediacy, not from a step or two back from the action, or from the observer's viewpoint. Don't make the mistake of being an observer - be a fully participating member of the group for maximum effect.

The aims of the personal development component of training can include:

• Helping trainees understand the client role. This gives us exposure to and insight into the range of possible feelings experienced by clients, including an appreciation of the power dynamics of helping relationships.

• Being a client or subjecting ourselves to a group personal development process gives evidence that we trust the counselling process. Would you go to a dentist who i) only went to the dentist when they had raging toothache, ii) didn't trust dentists and iii) thought that dentistry was only 'OK for those who needed it in an emergency'?

• Helping trainees develop an increased awareness of their *self* as an individual. We are better helpers if we understand ourselves better, with fewer 'blind spots' and unhelpful attitudes and prejudices.

• Securing commitment to ongoing personal and professional development. It is a requirement that professional helpers continually maintain their 'fitness' to practice (like an athlete being in training to maintain peak performance).

• Group PD is a good way of understanding that helping has a social and relationship context and that counselling has to work with complex socially constructed meanings, not just individual worlds. Skills of negotiation, appreciation of consensus and group vs individual needs can all be explored.

When PD is done in a group setting, all of the issues, both positive and negative, that arise in group learning will also be present. This means that the whole experience can add up to something quite momentous or at times over (or under) -whelming. Skilful facilitation of this group work is essential, yet at the same time, all group members must remember that there is a collective and individual responsibility for what happens in the group.

Student-Centred Learning

This is not a new idea and is not practised on all counselling training courses. However, many courses do nod in the direction of student-centred education for a whole bunch of reasons, only some of which may be rooted in the philosophical basis of the course. It might be reasonable, for example, to assume that any course which promotes a model of counselling in which the impetus for client change comes from within the client, practices some degree of student self-managed learning.

It is also reasonable to expect a humanistic, especially person-centred course to implement student centred learning as far as it is able because of the deep connection with person-centred therapy, not because it is a fashionable idea. Back in 1951 Carl Rogers was writing about student centred teaching and noted that even then it was a rediscovery of effective principles which had already been stated by others. He also noted that the nature of the process was facilitating learning, not teaching since

' A person learns significantly only those things which he perceives as being involved in the maintenance of, or enhancement of, the structure of self.' p.389 'Client Centered Therapy' 1951

He then outlined the conditions which needed to be in place before such self-directed and self-managed learning was likely to take place:

• *'an acceptant climate'* p.389 ibid.

- *' development of individual and group purposes'* p.389 ibid.
- tutors that flexibly facilitate different stages of learning
- a focus on self and peer evaluation

Students of the person-centred approach will probably be familiar with these ideas, but students on other courses might find them incomprehensible, alien or just plain wrong thinking. Clearly a course should choose a learning method and principles that are in harmony with the theoretical approach at the centre of the course. If you find yourself in a course which appears to promote or claims to provide student-centred learning, here are some questions you might find worth asking yourself, your fellow trainees or your tutors:

- *Why* does the course espouse student-centred learning? What is so good about it?
- *How* does it fit with the core theoretical model of the course?
- *In what ways* does the course implement student-centred learning? Do you have self assessed assignments, peer assessed assignments? Can the students determine the content and method of the sessions?
- *Are* there opportunities to discuss the whole group learning process, your individual learning process and how the two interact (such as community meetings)?

Tutors should be able to answer these questions by relating the course structure to a theory of counselling or a theory of education. On the one hand, a laissez-faire or 'anything goes' approach may not be acceptable to you. On the other hand, two of the skills of counselling are firstly, to be able to assess your self - your own development and your performance. Secondly is the ability to assess other peoples growth and state of being. So it is easy to see why so many courses, whether they are person-centred or not, involve a reasonable amount of self- and peer-evaluation and /or assessment.

Genuine student-centred learning can be a disturbing experience for a number of course participants. Most of us have had experiences of education that can best be described as 'traditional'. When the tutors do not take responsibility for our learning, and instead expect us to identify our own learning needs, set our own learning objectives, configure our own learning environment, manage our own learning pathway and assess our own achievement, we can feel rather abandoned even to the point of believing that the tutors have completely abdicated their role.

These challenges should be facilitated on a person-centred course and participants should be supported and challenged, not abandoned. This does not mean, however, that in our anxiety, we may not *feel abandoned*. On a person-centred course, we might reasonably expect these feelings of anxiety and abandonment to be heard respectfully, not batted back to us as 'our stuff'.

At the end of a course that puts student-centred learning at the centre of the educational experience, we might find participants experiencing a greater sense of personal achievement and they might have a greater sense of personal relevance in their learning, i.e. that they *did it themselves* - not *in spite of* the trainers, as I have sometimes heard participants complain, but *facilitated by them.*

Did you know

what psychologists have found out about learning?

1

Learning and memory are linked in much the same way that attention and perception (see pages 51 & 45) are linked, except that I can say without fear of contradiction that you cannot remember something that you have not learned. When we are thinking about studying, the issue is, 'What are the best ways of getting information (ideas and understandings) into our system and how can we improve recall and recognition - the two processes by which we attempt to get the information back out of our system?' What is clear from research is that it is sensible to look at this *information processing system* as a whole working unit. How information is learned affects how it will be stored and that affects how it can be recalled or used in recognition.

Learning by association

The kind of learning first described at the turn of the century and developed by behaviourist psychologists consists of events being linked by association. Pavolv discovered that reflexes and other involuntary responses (famously, the salivary reflex in dogs) can be linked by association with all kinds of external stimuli (bells, lights, etc.) and Thorndike discovered that animals could link simple deliberate or voluntary responses into chains if they were associated with a reward. Such learning is very simple indeed, so simple that insects, even the severed legs of insects, show a capability to learn in a similar way.

Another feature of this approach to learning is the understanding that small units or building blocks of learning can be stacked up into more complex patterns. The ideas underpinning an appreciation of this type of learning have been developed into sophisticated explanations of much more complex learned behaviours. Central to this approach is the notion that learning happens in increments, or a series of small steps. If learning is to be successful it is better done in a series of easy to manage steps, each with a better chance of success than one huge lump of learning that may defeat us by its sheer size. This way our effort is rewarded by a sense of achievement at each stage.

What is also clear from this work is that reflexive responses such as anxiety can become associated with external stimuli (so fear can become associated with study settings or exam rooms) and poor study habits can, if accidentally rewarded, become entrenched behaviours. Many of us are victims of exam anxiety or general fear of failure if we have previously associated attempts to study and hand in work with criticism and failure.

Did you know   *what psychologists have found out about learning?*

Psychologists define learning as a 'relatively permanent change in behaviour', so what can be learned can be un-learned or re-learned. If we have come to associate fear or failure with exam rooms or studying in general, it is possible to re-learn an association that is more productive.

Learning sets
This, rather like *perceptual set* (see page 45,) is a state of readiness to learn a particular thing. This state of readiness is like learning a 'rule' and is sometimes referred to as 'learning to learn'. Experiments with monkeys (Harlow 1949) show that learning the rules of learning can look quite sophisticated, even when the rules of learning themselves are very simple indeed. Psychologists have demonstrated that learning sets can be disadvantageous too because we can very easily learn an unproductive set of rules. These then slow down learning or sometimes make it nigh on impossible to learn something.

State-dependent learning
In 1972, Overton showed that people under the influence of alcohol could remember things that had happened to them on similar occasions much more readily than when they had not been drinking. It seems likely that this finding might apply to other emotional states too, and it seems to work by providing a context for helping us to remember. This is similar to the external stimuli referred to in the sections above, with the additional factor of the internal stimulus of the emotional state itself, i.e. how you were *feeling* when you learned something or even *where you were* when you learned something.

How can we use these findings?
How you learn something will affect how easy or difficult it will be to remember, so get your learning environment right. The following are specific examples:

If you have had bad experiences as a child or teenager at school where you associate learning something new to failure, it is possible to break the association and re-learn that learning can be a success for you - but this won't be easy.

Learning itself has rules (see Chapter 3) and sometimes we learn rather daft, unhelpful rules. Understanding the learning process will help us learn useful rules rather than unproductive rules.

Learning in a given situation, associated with particular feeling will be best remembered in a similar situation with similar feelings. That is one reason why experiential learning is so powerful. We recognise the similarities in the setting in which we learned skills, e.g. a counselling role play, when we try to replay the skills in a real life setting with a real client.

Hints and Tips 2

1. Expect things to have changed since you were last in education. Methods in adult education are different from those used in schools.

2. Most of the course you are on will be conducted in groups and much of the learning will be *experiential*, or 'learning-by-doing.

3. You can't learn if you don't get involved. Be prepared to try things out, practice your skills in front of others, speak up and share your experience.

4. Take the opportunity afforded by group learning to observe other students and the way they learn. How do they cope with the new situation?

5. Don't be afraid to experiment with different ways of learning and being. You may not be used to active participation, so now is the time to be different.

6. You may be used to being silent in groups, you may be used to being the centre of attention in groups. You may not be used to being in groups at all. Whatever the case, you will be expected to share in the learning life of the group. This will involve listening to feedback on the way you are and changing the way you are used to doing things.

7. Avoid the tendency to compete in groups. Trainees are not being set against each other. You may have got this idea from school - it doesn't work like this in counselling training. If anything you'll be encouraged to co-operate.

8. Establish groundrules in the groups you'll be working in. You will feel safe and learn more that way.

9. Personal development can be shrouded in mystery on some courses. Don't worry, everyone will be in more-or-less the same boat.

10. Read any handouts on PD issued by the course tutors. Don't stay in the dark any longer than you have to.

11. Be sure you understand the learning methods used on the course and be sure you are happy with them, i.e. that they fit in with your preferred learning style. Ask the tutors to justify their educational methods if you have any doubts.

Getting Your Learning Environment Right

3

One of the tricks of successful study is to get things right. This will come as no surprise to you, I'm sure. In fact you may well think 'Yes of course, everyone knows that, but how do you know what's right?' My intention here is to suggest that there are several answers to this 'What is right?' question depending upon your viewpoint, and that in order to be successful on a counselling course you will have to look at things from more than one viewpoint. This isn't a complicated thing to do, but it may be a *new* way of doing things for you. As a matter of fact, you will specifically learn how to look at things from different points of view as a participant on a counselling course, so extending the idea to the area of studying should not be too difficult.

This brings me quickly on to another important point: you must be prepared to do things differently. You will learn that studying is not an 'art' or a 'gift', but a mix of understanding and practising the skills of studying, planning, hard work, fun, creative energy and excitement. You will probably have to learn how to do some of these (and some of us need to be reminded of how to have fun!) I can think of four main reasons why you might have to change or learn some new ways:

- One of the reasons we spend our time inefficiently and unproductively in study is because we repeat old bad habits.

- Another reason some of us struggle on courses in the 1990s is because the last time we did any sort of studying at all, the ideas and approaches to education were very different. I can remember reciting bits of the Bible in my junior school class sitting in rows. Your counselling course tutor will not ask you to memorise counselling theory this way, I'm sure, but you may find it quite challenging to discover just how much of the learning is left up to you.

- Yet another reason why we might not perform too well in assignments is that we don't fully understand either the nature of study nor what is required of us. In other words our expectations do not match reality. Successful studying is a bit like successful navigation. You need a good map of the territory, a travel plan and the confidence to ask if you think you might be lost.

- The final reason is that counselling courses often employ innovative assessment procedures which are intended to be congruent or in harmony with counselling as a process. These include group and individual peer assessment, personal learning journals and evaluating your skills on tape recordings of clients. Again, the area of *assessment* is likely to be challenging because some of us are not very used to it, even when it comes in a more 'traditional' package.

In order to be successful on your counselling course you will have to acquire new knowledge and skills and also change from using old *habits* to developing new more flexible *strategies*. This book will:

1. Help you identify the approaches and strategies you *currently* use.
2. Give you information about what ways of studying have been found to be effective by others.
3. Make suggestions, based on this information, regarding how you might change your habits to become more effective.
4. Look at the range of assessments used by counselling courses and how best to tackle them.
5. Give you some insight into the different viewpoints on the whole business of completing a counselling course.

What is a learning environment?

When you first read the chapter title, you may have a picture in your mind of a library or a classroom. I am using the term *learning environment* in a much wider sense than that. I would invite you to think of your learning environment as having three components.

Firstly there is your **internal** environment, or what is happening inside you when you are learning or trying to learn. Your personality, values, attitudes, and beliefs formed from past experiences of instruction, discovery and learning. This also includes how *you* best learn, why you are wanting to learn, what motivates you to do the course you are doing and how you reward yourself for learning.

Secondly there are the **learning relationships** you have with fellow course participants (or peers), your tutors and course facilitators, the person who supervises any counselling or counselling skills practice you do and any clients you might have. Each and all of these is a learning environment.

Thirdly there is the **external** environment, or the *place* or *places* in which your learning takes place. These will, of course, move around with you wherever you go and might include:
  • Some places in which you study:
    • college, institute or place the course meets,
    • library,
    • train or bus travelling to work or college,
    • a room or rooms in your home.
  • Some places in which you discuss counselling with tutors and fellow course participants:
    • the room in which your course meets,
    • the canteen, snack-bar or common room,
    • the pub,
    • your home or theirs.
  • Some places in which you contemplate counselling:
    • your home,
    • your car, the bus or train as you travel,
    • in bed at night or in the morning.
  • Some places in which you do counselling or practice counselling skills:
    • the place agency where you work,
    • your home,
    • college, institute or place the course meets.

We will look at each of these in turn and how you might try to bring about change or influence these environments to get the best learning out of each one. There is some overlap since they interact with each other, but we can make a start with our*selves*.

Learning environments and resources

Learning does not take place in a vacuum, there is always a context that will either help or hinder the process. It takes place inside a particular person (you in this instance) with a particular history, in particular relationships at a particular time in a particular place. It is not just you receiving knowledge from books and your tutor. The diagram below shows how you are at the centre of a network of resources for learning. Success can depend upon whether you recognise, claim and use as many of these resources as possible. (Not everyone has access to all of these resources, such as a space at home to study.)

External learning environment

College or institute: *facilities, ease of access, feeling of personal safety.* Rooms and accommodation: *comfortable seating, good equipment, feels 'safe' and 'yours'.* Course Structure: *lectures, personal development groups, tutorials, etc., and breaks.* Library and resources: *reasonable access to books and materials.* Home: *safe place for support and nurture.* A place to study at home: *space for undisturbed study.* Place you do your counselling or counselling skills practice: *safe comfortable space for clients.*

Learning relationships

Tutors: *information, advice and guidance, evaluation and support.* Peers: *sharing experiences, receiving feedback and support.* Clients: d*eveloping counselling and professional skills plus feedback and personal development.* Supervisor: r*estoration, support and developing professional and ethical standards.* Family and friends: *support and nurturing during your course.*

You and your internal learning environment

Past experience of discovery, learning and instruction; success and failure.

Personality and preferences.

Attitudes, values and beliefs

Your internal *learning environment*

Your counselling course will undoubtedly have a component related to self-awareness. Now, whatever you understand by this term, few students ever imagine that it could include looking at *understanding how you learn best.* This section is concerned with helping you find out what makes you tick in terms of learning and studying. (It is then up to you whether you put any of the findings into practice.)

It should go without saying that each of us will study in our own way. Often we have not learned this in any systematic way, but rather through a series of accidental successes or failures which have given us a set of idiosyncratic beliefs and methods that are probably not far short of superstitions. Some of these superstitions will be based on 'something nasty happening in the geography class when we were young', some on myths about how to study and some will be based on our own preferences for the way *we* learn best. The panel below and the activity on page 33 will help you identify some myths and superstitions, and explore your personal preferences. The aim is to help increase your self-awareness when it comes to studying and learning.

You may have guessed as you were reading through the list of myths and superstitions that none of them is true; that's why I'm referring to them as myths

Myths and Superstitions

The perfect student:

• Reads every book and journal on the reading list from cover to cover.
• Understands and remembers everything in lectures, seminars and books straight away with no effort.
• Writes a brilliant essay at the first attempt, well before the deadline.
• Is never anxious about their performance.
• Has no time for fun, family or social life.

Tutors:

• Are always fair and consistent when marking work.
• Never give hints and tips about how to tackle assignments.
• Know everything about counselling - have read all the books on the reading list, read each edition of 'Counselling' from cover to cover.
• Never have any doubts about how to mark a piece of work and never make a mistake.
• Try to knock marks off wherever possible.

Study success in general:

• Marks are given in proportion to the amount written - the more you write, the more marks you get.
• Put lots of time in - just sit down with the books in front of you, it doesn't matter if you don't understand it.
• You should always do everything the tutor says without question because they know best.
• You will be seen as a troublemaker if you ask questions.

Activity

Who is responsible for my learning on my counselling course?

In this chapter we look at some of the distinctive features of the learning process in counselling training. Depending upon your past experience in education, including how long ago it was that you were last in the role of 'pupil', 'student' or 'trainee', you will have different expectations of what counselling training will be like. Your expectations will also depend upon the theoretical orientation of the course; person-centred, cognitive, psychodynamic, etc. This questionnaire should get you thinking about how counselling training might compare with these expectations. The aim is to raise your awareness...

Compared to your last experience in education as a 'student', do you think you will be expected to take *less, the same, more* or *total* responsibility for the activity or your learning:

	less	same	more	total
• Which assignments to do.				
• How much time to spend on 'homework' or private study.				
• Whether to attend class or not.				
• Whether your fellow students should pass or fail.				
• Where to locate resources and learning materials.				
• Which learning resources (books, etc) are most useful and appropriate.				
• Deciding how well you are doing on the course.				
• Whether you should pass or fail.				
• When to complete assignments, i.e. on time, or not.				
• Which areas of the course to put most effort into.				

and superstitions. Yet it is surprising how many of us either *believe* that some or all of them are true, or even though we *know* that they're daft ideas, we *behave* as though they were true. One of the aims of this book is to help us all (me included) to move away from the mythology of learning and study and discover what is really true for each of us.

You may be wondering what myths and superstitions I believe. Well not long ago I was a student on a personnel management course and, even though I told myself that I should know better, I expected the tutors to be fair and consistent in their marking, that I would be seen as a troublemaker if I asked questions, and that I should be able to write a brilliant essay at my first attempt. Even now as a tutor it is difficult for me to shrug off the expectations that I should know everything about counselling and that I must read everything that has ever been published on the subject.

It is time to start debunking some of these myths and set ourselves free to discover the best ways of learning for ourselves. I will not go through each myth and superstition in turn, except to say that one giveaway is the tendency to use absolute words like 'must', 'should', always, and 'never'. *Complete* dedication, *absolute* understanding, *total* recall are all unreasonable aims.

There are two basic ways of understanding the process of studying. They relate to the myths and superstitions in the panel on page 24. Which of the following categories do you fit into best?

• Some students believe that knowledge consists of an increasing number of 'correct' answers and that tutors supply knowledge in the form of lots of 'correct' ways of doing things.

  • These students also believe that essays and exams should be tackled by writing down as many of these 'correct' answers as possible to guarantee the maximum possible mark.
  • Such students then think that assessment is a perfect system of marking these 'correct' answers by infallible markers.
  • These students will tend to see a tutor's suggestions as 'rules' and follow these 'rules' to the letter, whether they are helpful or not.
  • This rather mechanical view of learning and assessment is generally held by the *less successful* students.

• Other students, on the other hand, know that what is 'correct' will vary from situation to situation, even from tutor to tutor, each presenting a different viewpoint, none of which will be absolutely correct.

  • Exams and essays then will involve discussion of different perspectives, offering your own viewpoint and experiences.
  • To these students marking is a fallible process and may be different from tutor to tutor. Such students will ask tutors for hints and tips, will listen carefully to guidance on how to answer questions (but not follow them as though suggestions were 'rules') and be selective in their preparation as a result.
  • These students look for clues in the way tutors behave and speak to get an idea about what is required.
  • This more flexible view of learning and assessment is generally held by the *more successful* students.

It doesn't matter what level or stage of counselling

Activity - The way *you* prefer to study and learn

Look at the following questions and statements about personal qualities, habits and preferred ways of learning. Which ones do you think apply to you? The questions and statements are written to get you thinking actively about you and your *internal learning environment*. Whilst the answers are important, we will not be trying to *diagnose* anything from them - simply note your answers and absorb them as personal feedback.

Personal motivation

• Why am I doing this course? (Do any of these fit?)

- It is my dream come true.
- I want to be a professional counsellor.
- I was sent by my employer, but I don't really see the point.
- I've been counselling for years and I need the qualification for my CV.
- I want to improve my social life.
- Although I'm not a counsellor, counselling skills will help me in my job.
- Other reason(s)

• I am looking forward to this counselling course.

• I don't know how I'm going to fit this course in with all my other commitments.

• I really enjoy studying.

• I am happy with the way I study and I think that the effort I put into studying is rewarded by good results.

• I have made sacrifices to be on this course, so I'm going to make damned sure that I pass.

The way I work

• I generally speaking finish the projects I start.

• I get distracted easily when studying.

• I find it difficult to start a piece of work, but am OK once I get going.

• I find it easy to start but can never seem to find a way to finish.

• Once I get behind, I give up.

• I am a perfectionist; never satisfied or not wanting to hand work in because I think it's not good enough.

• I always leave things to the last minute - I work much better that way.

• I can't get anything done unless I plan it carefully first and give myself plenty of time - otherwise I panic.

• I have to have complete and utter quiet when I work - no disturbances at all.

• I work much better with the TV or Radio on.

• I can only concentrate for short periods, then I just drift off.

• I always worry that I'm not reading or studying the right thing, so I flit from book to book or topic to topic and never seem to get anywhere.

training you are at. Your study habits and internal learning environment will follow you and affect the way you go about things, the results you achieve and the satisfaction (or disappointment) you experience. This is your opportunity for changing either your habits so that they fit in with the real world of studying counselling, or negotiating changes in the course to fit in with you. (It would be wonderful but unreasonable to expect that your counselling course could simple adjust its requirements to accommodate all of your quirks and learning needs.)

Your learning relationships

The diagram on page 29 indicates a number of different learning relationships. I will start by looking at the sort of relationship you, the course participant, have with the college or institute and educational practices in general. This relationship is governed by three things:

1. Your past experience of education - what you have come to expect.
2. The college's attitude towards students (this can be evidenced in a number of ways and includes, to some extent, the tutors' attitudes towards students).
3. Your personal power as an adult learner, and the degree to which this is acknowledged and enhanced by the special nature of counselling courses.

Since counselling training is about *listening, respect, openness, being genuine, understanding power in relationships and helping people change and grow* it would be reasonable to expect that tutors would hold some of these values at the heart of the course process and that they would be evident in the way the course operates as a learning environment. Many courses offer some *student-led* components as one

way of acknowledging this, whilst others offer an element of *peer assessment*. Still others allow students to negotiate some elements of assessment.

At the same time, courses need to establish and maintain a standard, especially at Diploma level, where if the course hours are sufficient (more than 300) you would be expecting to be trained to the level of professional counsellor. It is important that courses pass only those people up to the standard, and fail only those people not up to the standard. This is a difficult line to tread; not being too strict nor too lenient. How can a course team do this and still acknowledge the very personal and human aspects of learning counselling or counselling skills?

Doing it *your* way - your rights as a student

For many adult learners, the last experience of education was school where we simply did as we were told without question, where students' questions were at best an irritation, where the curriculum was non-negotiable, where what we learned were 'facts' and lengthy discussion was not encouraged and personal experiences not seen as valid.

Doing counselling training will be different for a few reasons:

Firstly, we are now adult learners and adults have personal requirements for respectful treatment. (That is not to say that teenage learners are any less deserving of respect, but the reality of life is that they simply either are not offered respect or do not experience it.) *Secondly,* counselling training is about developing our understanding of the helping qualities of human relationships and the best way

Your rights as a student:
Training Contracts

Many colleges and training organisations take your rights seriously by providing a learning contract. It is a list of the things they promise to provide, and a list of the things they expect from you. Here is a typical list giving certain assurances which can be checked out as your training proceeds.

If you have applied for one of our courses we will
• Treat your application fairly, seriously and with respect regardless of your race, colour, religion, age, sexual orientation or class.
• Interview you if you require an interview.
• Provide you with information about our college/organisation.
• Keep all your application details confidential.
• Destroy our records of your application(s) if you do not enrol for one of our courses, if you wish us to.

If you are a student we will
• Provide you with a copy of our complaints and appeals procedure.
• Explain the workings of our Students' Union and Departmental Meetings and other ways in which you can influence the way we run our courses.
• Treat you and your training seriously and with respect regardless of your race, colour, religion, age, sexual orientation or class.
• Provide you with the teaching contact hours indicated in the course publicity.
• Provide an environment in which together with the tutors and other students, you can share in the responsibility of creating your own safe learning space.
• Provide high quality teaching accommodation exclusively dedicated to your course. None of the accommodation will be shared. You will not be asked to move.
• Mark your work promptly and give you fair and constructive feedback on it.
• Give regular feedback on your progress on your course. In most cases this is built into the programme.
• Provide access to our library of books and training materials.

When you leave us we will
• On request, provide fair and accurate references for jobs or other education applications.
• On request, give you an interview in which we will help you plan your next move in counselling.

of doing this is to use the relationships 'in hand' so-to-speak. So there will be much discussion and sharing of personal experiences of past and present helping through relationships.

Thirdly, counselling concerns itself with personal empowerment, so counselling courses try to model this to some extent by giving participants a degree of power and responsibility over their own learning. This is nearly always very challenging since, due to the first point above, most of us are just not used to self-determination in learning settings.

Finally, there is a new, *customer-centred* culture in public services including education. In the 1990s we are much more likely to have promises made (at least that we will not be discriminated against on the basis of colour, religion, gender etc.) and asked for our opinion to help improve future provision or to evaluate existing provision etc.

It sometimes proves difficult to manage the challenge of taking responsibility for our own learning given that so much seems to have changed in education and counselling training is so different from an academic subject. At the same time it is a very exciting challenge, since we really do have the opportunity of integrating learning that has particular personal significance. This is very close to the change we are trying to facilitate in others when we use counselling skills.

Some of the ways in which we might be invited to take personal responsibility for our learning are:

• To monitor it daily or weekly by keeping a *personal learning journal*. The majority of courses now use personal journals.

• To take part in regular *community meetings* which can be structured or unstructured. These are particularly favoured on person-centred courses.

• *Self-evaluation* or assessment. We may be asked to evaluate our own work - particularly our counselling skills performance to see if we can appreciate the difference between effective and ineffective use of skills in our own work. There will be more on this throughout the book.

• *Personal tutorials* are an opportunity not only to receive feedback from tutors but also to say what your personal learning needs are and how the course is or isn't meeting them. Also you can explain how your personal circumstances may require special consideration, from special learning needs through to family illness or personal crisis.

• Through *course evaluation*. We may be asked to fill in course evaluation sheets where our comments, positive and negative, will be used to improve course provision. This is a golden opportunity, so don't be afraid of putting down what you really think.

• *Student contracts* or *learning contracts* are increasingly used by colleges and institutes as evidence of the quality of their provision. Rather like a Customers' Charter, they are promises of a certain level and standard of service. If you are offered one, you could see that it is kept to through some of the above methods. See page 35.

Doing it *their* way - reasonable course requirements
All readers will know that rights do not come without

responsibilities. As students it is our responsibility to stay within the rules laid down by the organisation.

We expect you to:
• Give an honest account of your experience and qualifications at application.
• Commit yourself to attending at least 80% of the time on your course.
• Be prepared to take your training commitment seriously.
• Hand your work in on time, or negotiate extensions with your tutor.
• Not behave in racist, sexist or otherwise oppressive or abusive ways.
• Not to smoke on college premises other than in designated areas.
• Agree to abide by college rules and regulations.

This example of the students' responsibilities in a counselling course contract gives some idea of what might be reasonable from an organisation's point of view. In addition to this students should expect to be told the titles and nature of any assignments and the dates they are due. Assessment and assignments are looked at more fully in Chapter 5.

Learning from and with tutors

Learning relationships with the tutors in training are of central importance. In counselling training it is not uncommon for tutors to participate in exercises and contribute their own personal material to discussions. Learning relationships in adult education in general tend to be less formal than, for example, at school. These learning relationships stand a good chance of being coloured by our previous experiences, particularly our brushes with authority. It is easy to become rebellious, angry, dependent on, or infatuated with tutors because they are not behaving in the traditional way we expect tutors to behave:

• *Do not* expect tutors to be detached and distant (I think of my old headteacher as detached and distant). On a counselling course we may find that the tutors *model* the good practice of the counselling approach that the course is based on. (So tutors on a person-centred course should be expected to be non-judgemental, warm, empathic and genuine.)
• *Do* expect tutors to keep within their role and not become *friends* during the course (although this may happen afterwards, especially if, as sometimes happens, past students become colleagues.)
• *Do* expect tutors to be fair and consistent in their assessment of your work - there is usually a system of double-marking to avoid accidental unfair marking. At the same time as expecting to receive fair treatment, do not be afraid to challenge grades if you think your work has been misunderstood. You can always have it marked by another tutor or the external examiner if there is a problem. There is more on these safeguards on pp 85-89 in Chapter 5.

Learning from and with peers

In counselling training we use relationships between course participants as one of the main foci of learning. Particular use of these relationships is made in counselling skills development when participants work in twos and threes practising counselling skills

- often using audio or video tape to record the 'session'. In order to learn by doing in this way both 'counsellor' and 'client' need to take a few risks and in order to do this they will need to feel safe. We can all expect to feel anxious or embarrassed in such settings so feeling supported by our peers in essential to providing a safe, supportive learning environment.

We might think that feeling safe in learning situations would simply be a matter of getting to know the others in our group. Although this *is* an important ingredient, we should be ready for the unexpected:

- We might not like the people we are working with. (There is no rule that says we *must* get on with the other people on our course.) We might have different views, beliefs or values from other people or maybe they remind us of someone we don't like. Such dislike can lead to us not feeling like taking risks in front of the others in the group.
- We might like the people we are working with *too much*. In this event we might find it difficult to give them feedback that is constructive. We might forsake constructive negative feedback for mutual back-slapping.

Fortunately, since we are hoping to learn about helping in human relationships, these likes and dislikes are more grist to the mill. Hopefully the course will provide opportunities where students will be able to learn how to understand these relationship dynamics rather than be victims of them.

Relationships with peers gives us other valuable opportunities to 'learn by doing' in the sense that we can practise the kind of qualities we need to

demonstrate with clients and those we are trying to help, with our fellow course participants:

- Understanding the worlds of those we do not get on with too well.
- Being open and genuine in relationships with our peers in training is a valuable, some would say essential, attribute, even though it will sometimes be difficult.
- Remaining non-judgemental and respectful, even though we hold very different views.

Groundrules and contracts

Another ingredient in the process of creating a safe learning environment through relationships is to set some groundrules. The idea of groundrules is helpful in almost any situation where people need to feel safe, whether it be helping using counselling skills, counselling or learning about counselling. We need to know, for instance:

- whether what we say and do will be reported to others;
- whether we will be judged (this is important on a course since we would not want tutors to encourage us to be open and then judge us negatively when we are);
- whether whatever we say and do will be treated with respect.

In addition to these conditions, we might want to make sure that, for example,

- we will not be interrupted;
- no-one will smoke during the session (or that smoking is positively permitted);
- participants will arrive on time and stay till the end.

Sometimes groundrules can be formalised in a

contract between participants (tutors included) and they may be written down or put up on the wall as a reminder of what was agreed. Here is an example of a skills group contract.

Our skills group contract

• We want commitment:
    1. Give notice if you can't attend.
    2. Arrive in good time to start.
    3. Keep good time at breaktime.
• We give permission for self-disclosure for self and skills development.
• We want to *give* honest, sensitive, constructive feedback.
• We want to *be open to* all feedback, especially challenging feedback.
• Start with a check-in, finish with a check-out.
• Treat all work with respect, as though it were our own.
• Confidentiality: nothing goes outside this group, not even to partners, without permission.
• 'Client' says what happens to any tapes - whether they're played or not.
• No smoking

As I have mentioned, in counselling skills and diploma courses it is common practise to expect trainees to work in twos and threes to practise counselling skills. One person is the talker or client, another is the listener or counsellor and if necessary there will be a third person in the role of observer. These learning/helping relationships need careful management for a number of reasons.

• It is important to establish working priorities: what is most important here - the needs of the talker or the learning needs of the listener?
• The talker needs to know and understand that the listener is a novice counsellor in training and will probably make 'mistakes'. (It will not, therefore, be appropriate to bring deep issues to the session.)
• Unless you make an arrangement to stay together as a pair for a few weeks, these sessions will be a succession of 'first interviews' and you will not get any idea of the progression of a helping relationship.
• Boundaries need to be carefully set, e.g. time allowed, confidentiality, etc., especially if the sessions are tape recorded for playback and review in the presence of other trainees and tutors, e.g.
    • Who 'owns' the material on the tape, the talker or the listener?
    • Can the talker ask that the tape be erased, and can they ask this at any point - even some time later?
    • Even though it may be an important tape for the listener's course assessment, can the talker refuse permission for its use?

Setting working groundrules for these sessions is a good way of ensuring that you make the most of this learning opportunity without hurting yourself or those you are working with. When groundrules are set so that everyone feels safe, a great deal of positive learning can take place.

Getting support from friends and family

Fitting a demanding training course into family and work commitments can be difficult. Not only does it take up time to attend the course, but also it means spending time reading and preparing assignments. If you are on a diploma course it also means taking time to see clients (this may be extra to your normal working hours.) This adds up to a lot of extra effort on everyone's part to make way for your course. Having the support of colleagues, family and friends just to make your training possible at a logistical level is essential. They will have to make way for your training in a number of ways, they may have to take on extra work to make up for your absence, whether it's extra jobs at work, or doing the dishes at home.

In addition to the practicalities, there is a high probability that you will change during the course. These changes can often put pressure on friendships, work and family relationships. It is this element of counselling training that we least bargain for and the one that has the potential for affecting us the most. There are no words of wisdom that will help other than to point out generally that forewarned is forearmed and seeking the active support of family and friends means that you must make contact with them. Don't forget your family and social life as you immerse yourself in your studies, see pages 34 & 35

Learning from clients and supervisors

As I have suggested earlier, peers acting in the role of client (albeit bringing their own real personal issues) can provide a wonderful learning opportunity. In addition to this is the learning which takes place in our helping relationships with real clients, and the supervision we get for this work whilst in training. The supervision of trainee counsellors is, in my view, a specialised activity with occasionally quite a different emphasis from the supervision of qualified counsellors.

Brigid Proctor and Francesca Inskipp have pioneered the idea of learning to be a good supervisee, that is, being able to make the best use of supervision from choosing your supervisor through to actually turning up for your first supervision session. Their publication *The Art, Craft and Tasks of Supervision, Part 1 Making the Most of Supervision,* is an excellent programme with text and tapes, taking beginning counsellors through the necessary steps towards their first supervision session and beyond. (Many seasoned professional counsellors have gained much through working through this material, myself included.)

Supervision, tutorial and peer support are the main guidelines by which trainees negotiate the tricky learning process provided by their counselling or counselling skills practice. I'm not sure who said that 'we get the clients we deserve' (that is to say, need, or can learn most from) but I've reflected on those words many times in the supervision of my own counselling practice. As trainee counsellors you have a powerful learning resource available if only you can use it. This type of learning is on the boundary between skills, understanding theory and an openness to personal development.

This section on learning relationships is drawn to a close with two personal accounts of counselling training. Tracey writes about her experiences during her diploma course and Martyn her husband gives us some insight into his struggles to stay with the big changes that were happening as a result of Tracey's training. These are real people's accounts, not vignettes invented to make a specific point.

Inside Story 1: *The Life Partnership and Family*
Staying together during counselling training

Tracey and Martyn Walshaw

Tracey's Story

Tracey followed her certificate in counselling skills with an intensive part-time diploma course. She worked part-time as a nurse in a psychiatric day-unit, has two children and her partner is Martyn. She writes about various aspects of the whole experience.

Workload

Balancing part time employment, coursework, time at college, personal study, therapy, supervision, being a partner, mother, friend, daughter, etc was a nightmare at times. I felt like an uncoordinated circus juggler, it was both impossible and possible at the same time. I remember my heartstrings (or was it guiltstrings?) pulling when my daughter said after working late one evening to meet diploma deadlines, 'I want a real mummy, not one that goes to school' and when my son asked if I could 'play out'. I tried to plan and be sensible but there was never enough time.

Course 'membership'

Being a course member on a diploma felt like heart and soul stuff. I'm sure its 'specialness' excluded other long-standing relationships. It felt at times that my peers (the chosen ones!) seemed to be the only people that understood what was going on for me. This was probably because the personal development work meant sharing things I'd never shared before without feeling judged or people being

Martyn's Story

Martyn was an unsuspecting engineer when Tracey started her counsellor training. He charts his thoughts and feelings, following Tracey's headings (as he did during her courses). He had his own life to lead at this time, but it became dominated by her learning, development and change.

Workload

I had to become more active as far as looking after the children was concerned, which I didn't mind, but it was stressful at times. I didn't know how much extra work the diploma would mean for me and all our lives. Trace either didn't know or chose not to tell me at the outset! When Trace was tired, fraught, preoccupied or distant, I sometimes felt the course was taking her away from us. I came to hate how she left all her academic work to the last minute - early hours of the morning stuff, then having the cheek to get me up to retrieve it from the computer!

Course 'membership'

I couldn't understand these new relationships ...these people seemed more than just 'friends'. They'd spend all day together at college and what seemed like the rest of the week on the phone. (Watch out for the phone bills, partners of diploma students.) They seemed *very* close, seemed to be invading my territory. I guess I felt jealous at times. Sometimes Trace was so full of it she seemed

Inside Story 1: *The Life Partnership and Family*

Staying together during counselling training (*continued*)

Tracey's story ...continued

outraged at what I was saying. I'd come home bursting with stuff and have to put it on hold when I was met at the door by my daughter wanting to go to bed because 'Daddy doesn't read the same stories as you Mummy.' (Press the *on hold* button and re-enter my 'other life' - so there was life other than the diploma!) Getting the balance right was difficult if not impossible and downright exhausting.

Personal development and change

This was the major rocket launched in our lives by the diploma. Sometimes when I called 'Major Tom to ground control' *there was no ground control!* It was the start of a journey of life change and personal challenge for me. In personal therapy and the personal development group on the course I began to see through some of the fog in my life. I know my friends and family struggled with my changes and saw me as 'selfish', 'indulgent' and 'neglecting the children' or just 'she's strange - she's on one of those counselling courses!'. Even though it was stormy, I felt I had support from Martyn. I felt very lucky in this respect, since I am sure not all partners are as 'up for it' as Martyn was and continues to be.

Change has consequences and the consequences were momentous. The change in me disrupted all the major relationships in my life. Previously well established patterns of behaviour were upturned and redefined. Sometimes I was very wobbly as I turned over yet another stone to find another load

Martyn's story ...continued

obsessed, everything seemed to revolve around the course. I'm only an engineer - I didn't understand (or, at times, didn't particularly want to) and to me it seemed more than a course. It encroached on *my* life as well - this was unexpected and unwelcome at the time. I tried to understand but at times it was simply too stressful on our lives for me to do anything other than just endure it.

Personal development and change

Yes, I knew I had to see it through, to get a grasp of what she was doing, but I was terrified that she'd change from the Trace I'd known for all these years to who knows what! I saw her changing in other relationships and I think it was then that I first became frightened that she might change towards me, not want me any more, leave me behind! It didn't feel negative or bad, this change in her, just that it was making her different. I did feel resentful at times about her 'enjoying' this new self she'd found, and I was envious too. Often I just wanted it all to stop and for life to return to how it had been. I often got a lot of pessimistic gip from my colleagues and resorted to reassuring myself that we really did have a good relationship and that we would survive. I just stuck my head in the sand and hoped it would all go away...but of course it didn't.

I felt that Trace had changed without asking me and was leaving me behind - and I didn't want to be left! I could understand for the first time how other people's relationships founder when one of

Inside Story 1: *The Life Partnership and Family*

Staying together during counselling training *(continued)*

Tracey's story ...continued

of personal work underneath it. I remember Martyn once saying, 'If it's so bloody awful why do you do it?' My answer, of course, was 'It's the process' which made it about as clear as mud to Martyn and must have infuriated him because there were times when I seemed to be drowning in 'counselling speak'. Indeed, *I* often wanted to scream 'Stuff the bloody process!' But personal development work became a way of being. Once I'd started I was off on the path to...wherever. The genie could not be put back into the bottle.

Would I do it again and how could it have been better?

Yes, without hesitation, but I would try to do it a little differently with the magical gift of hindsight. Firstly, I would work harder at getting the balance between home life and 'diploma life' right - probably by trying to include Martyn more. I think I had *some* idea that he might find the personal development work difficult, but I still chose not to share my hopes and fears about it with him in case he withdrew his support totally. I guess I had the attitude of 'Well once I'm on the course, he'll have to work it through...and thank heaven he did! You can never be prepared for what personal development and change can bring, but it might have been better to let Martyn know that he'd have to expect the unexpected.

Martyn's story ...continued

the partners changes and the other doesn't want to understand. Although I realised *I* had to do something, admitting that it was *me* that had to change too was very hard. I was frightened to take the first step, even though I was living with a trainee counsellor, I didn't want to accept that counselling might help. After much agonising (yes, it was agony!), I went to see a counsellor. The minute I was there I found that there was no reason to be frightened by it although at times it was difficult and uncomfortable, opening up a new area of me that I didn't know about

Would I do it again and how could it have been better?

Counselling courses should carry a 'Government Health Warning'. If I had had more information about what the personal development work might have involved, it might not have come as such a shock, but I realise as I say this, that it might still have been a shock. Can you really prepare for the totally unexpected? The course gave out loads of information about the academic work, so I felt reasonably prepared for the workload and the stresses involved. But believe me partners-of-diploma-students, it is the PD work that is the killer - and boy, was I unprepared for it - it nearly killed me.

Would I support Trace again after all of this? The answer has to be 'Yes'. It was hard work, stormy, interesting and bloody frustrating at times, but Tracey is happier and that makes me happier too.

Your external *learning environment*

The environment we study in is a resource which can help or hinder our efforts to study. There can be no doubt that we experience some environments as more conducive to study than others. Whilst some of this is our own personal choice, prejudices and preferences, it is also true that some environments are intrinsically less suitable for study. It is also true that another personal factor comes into play on this issue, that of opportunity and accessibility of environments as resources. The purpose of this section is to look at the environment as a resource and to see how we might be able to maximise its usefulness and our effectiveness.

When I talk about your *external learning environment* I mean not only the buildings and rooms within which we meet or sit by ourselves with the intention of learning about counselling, but also the other things external to us that support our learning such as the structure of the course and learning support facilities such as libraries and course equipment. To some extent we take our learning environment around with us, like a mini weather-system (I can see a cartoon character walking down the road with a cloud raining on her head whilst the sun shines everywhere else). This bubble that follows us everywhere is so strong that some people can study literally anywhere, on the bus, train or tube, in bed, at meal times or whilst the TV is on, oblivious to anything going on around them They are in a world of their own. For those few people, the bulk of this chapter will have little to offer other than to let them know how the other 99% of us have to struggle to get our external learning environment right before we can learn effectively.

Course Structure

What should students look for in terms of course structure? There are no 'recommended' ways of putting together counselling training except that three strands of learning should be knotted together in some way or another.

- Theory (including professional and ethical issues at diploma level).
- Skills development (including supervised client practice at diploma level).
- Personal development (including personal therapy if required by your course).

Whilst there are no 'recommended' ways of structuring this learning, it is wise to look beyond the course towards your future as a counsellor or counselling skills practitioner. For instance, many counsellors-in-training have Registration as a counsellor via Accredited Counsellor Status with the British Association for Counselling as their professional goal. (If you are unfamiliar with these terms, ask your tutor or contact BAC.) So what are the Criteria for Accreditation as a counsellor? Firstly it is necessary to have completed 450 hours of training, and secondly it is necessary to have completed 450 hours of supervised counselling practice over a minimum of 3 years post-qualification. (There are various ways that this can be achieved, for details contact BAC at the address given on page 160.)

The first requirement is of interest to us here, since it would be wise to plan training that will meet these criteria. The training must not only be 450 hours in duration, but should also be split into 200 hours skills training and 250 hours counselling theory. If Accreditation is your aim, make sure your course

Did you know...

what psychologists have found out about perception?

2

Perception is not simply seeing things, it is the interpretation and giving meaning to all sensations. Since understanding is at the heart of the perceptual process, it has relevance to studying in general and studying counselling in particular. Much of the time spent developing counselling skills is the effort to communicate our understanding of the client's world. Like so many human processes, perception is active and constructive. We are continually trying to invest our sensations with meaning and form; we put order into the world where there is none, we complete incomplete sensations to make a meaningful whole, we have strong expectations about what will happen next and we are confused when it doesn't.

Perceptual set

When psychologists talk about 'set', they mean a state of predisposition or readiness to do something. Perceptual set, then, is a state of readiness to perceive certain kinds of things, i.e. to make *particular* interpretations of our sensory information rather than others. Sets can be generated in a number of ways, the most usual being through expectation. It is easier to have your expectations fulfilled than not, even at a perceptual level humans seem to limit uncertainty in this way. In 1955 Bruner and Minturn demonstrated this in a famous experiment in which they showed different

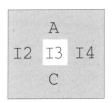

groups of people a series of either numbers or letters. they then showed the groups some ambiguous figures which could be seen as either a number or a letter, but was in fact, neither. Those who were shown letters, saw the ambiguous figures as letters and those who were shown numbers saw them as numbers. This simple demonstration shows how powerful and basic the tendency to have a 'set' is.

How can we use this finding?

It is difficult to counteract the powerful expectations we might have, but it is possible to be aware that we might, just might be blinkered in the way we are approaching understanding something. It helps to let go of preconceived ideas if we wish to understand some new material, whether it be some aspect of theory in a book or whether it is a privileged view into a client's private world. Try looking afresh rather than according to your expectations. The chances are you will only get your expectations met.

will help you meet these criteria.

In addition to the number of hours and how they are distributed, it makes sense to look at whether the hours of attendance are '*you*ser friendly', that is to say, do they fit *you*? For example, the following concerns might be important to you:

- Are there sufficient breaks?
- Are these included in lesson time?
- Is there community time when course issues can be discussed?
- Is there enough time to get done what you are expected to get done?
- Is there individual tutorial time when you can talk to tutors without harassing them during their breaks?
- What other questions would you need to have answered about course structure?

It is not reasonable to expect that a course should tailor its structure to meet your needs, but at the same time it is reasonable to expect that the course structure is sound, well thought out, appropriate for the learning aims and justifiable. It is also reasonable to expect that tutors will value feedback on the course structure since they will undoubtedly be seeking continual improvements. If the course leans towards being student-led or person-centred, then you can expect some greater say in how the course hours are arranged and the content of some of the sessions.

Training equipment and facilities

The major concern in counselling training is to learn about human relationships and this is done both in theory and practice. A decreasing minority of trainers would argue that the only resources we need to learn counselling in practice, are human beings in relationships, ourselves and a skilled facilitator. At very basic levels of training, this might be acceptable, but for training to a professional standard, some equipment is desirable. It is increasingly accepted that technology in the form of audio and video tape recorders not only speed the learning process up at diploma level, but actually enrich and deepen it, giving us personal feedback that is simply not available in any other way.

- An 'introduction to counselling' course is likely to achieve its aims fairly comfortably without recording equipment. The skill of the facilitators is paramount and much of the learning at this level is achieved through self-awareness and skills development exercises, role-plays and discussion.
- On a certificate or counselling skills course, the emphasis is frequently on *skills* and this is where recording equipment is most useful. The opportunity of seeing and/or hearing yourself and being able to evaluate your skills and get direct feedback from peers and tutors is the core of successful skills development. Whilst good skills development is possible without recording equipment, it is more difficult, likely to be less rigorous and requires a higher staff-student ratio if skills development is to be properly monitored and facilitated.
- Learning the advanced therapeutic techniques and professional skills associated with being a counsellor is very difficult without recording your performance and reviewing it with feedback from an experienced tutor. Practising therapeutic skills, either with fellow trainees as clients, or 'real' clients is almost bound to be an

essential course component at diploma level and learning in this way is enhanced by video recording, playback and review. Other useful technology includes good quality audiotape playback machines. These can greatly enhance the playback sound quality of tapes you may have made of sessions with clients.

Many courses spend some time exploring the use of creative arts methods in counselling, so having art materials available for some, or in some cases, all of the sessions is an important facility. A reasonable stock of paints, crayons, clay, paper etc. is necessary if creative work is a part of the syllabus. Even if a course does not include creative arts approaches,

there still should be a good supply of flipchart paper, flipchart stands, scrap paper and pens etc. to supplement work in small discussion groups.

If you are attending a diploma or professional level training course, it may be that you will have to make tape recordings of client sessions using your own audio cassette tape recorder. You will almost certainly be expected to provide this equipment yourself and it is a good idea to spend some time experimenting with equipment before you buy. In the first place, it may be the case that you have a perfectly adequate cassette recorder, but in order to make good voice recordings you will need to buy or borrow a reasonable microphone. Finding the right combinations of equipment is a matter of practical investigation. Do not take sales assistants' advice, take your recorder into the shop and try out a few microphones. The most expensive will not always give you the best results. Remember to include the cost of purchasing this equipment (and tapes) when estimating the total cost of a course.

Accommodation

The latest educational technology will not improve your learning environment if you do not have the right rooms and spaces in which to use it. This applies at home as well as at the premises of the training organisation responsible for your course. There is a slightly different emphasis when looking at our needs for an appropriate study space at home, yet it is no less important. It is surprising how many of us complain when everything is not 'just so' at college, yet are prepared to work on our knees in front of the TV at home, even when we have the choice to do otherwise.

Activity - Facilities
This is best done in small groups or with a friend to help sort ideas out or make suggestions.

• Think about your learning aims for the course and write them down.
   • What facilities, equipment, audio visual aids or other educational resources do *you* need in order to achieve these aims?
   • Which of these are best provided yourself, and which can you *reasonably* expect the course to provide?
• Given that course resources rarely if ever *perfectly* match our needs:
   • How can you work with your peers to share limited resources?
   • How can you work positively with tutors to improve resources, their availability and distribution?

Accommodation at your place of training

There is, as always, an element of personal preference when looking at how we like our accommodation to be arranged. Some people like open airy rooms with lots of windows, whilst others prefer cosier working spaces. Whatever our personal preferences might be there are some important features of rooms for counselling training that we should consider:

• *Availability*: Can you get into the rooms you want when you want to? Do other people want to use them at the same time? Are you moved out of rooms into other rooms in the middle of a session?

• *Access*: Can wheelchairs get in and out easily? Are there awkward steps or narrow corridors? Can you get the rooms opened if the tutors are not there, or do you have to wait in the corridor?

• *Adequacy*: Are the rooms large enough? Are there enough seats? Are there white/blackboards etc? Is the room 'echoey'? Is there intrusive noise from outside?

• *Comfort*: Is the seating comfortable? Is the floor carpeted/OK to sit on? Can you see the white/blackboards easily from all parts of the room? Is the heating, lighting, ventilation etc OK?

• *Safety*: Do the rooms feel safe places to work? Are sessions prone to interruption by people looking for someone, seeking directions etc? Are your possessions secure?

• *Privacy*: Can people see in from outside? Can you be heard by others in the next room?

• *Useability*: Are you allowed to move furniture around, sit or lie on the floor (is it comfortable/carpeted?), make noise, pin or stick your work to the walls and leave it up (will it be there when you next use the room?)?

A place to study at home

Only a portion of our learning takes place when we are actually in our training group or with the tutors. Much of the learning takes place in 'the rest of our lives' whether that is watching the television, sitting in quiet contemplation, reading a novel, listening to music, reading a counselling text, writing an essay, talking with friends... the list of times and places is almost endless. Some of these moments of learning are accidental, some we deliberately set up. When we deliberately set up a learning opportunity at home, we will undoubtedly have considered the space in which we choose to do that work.

For some trainees, a special space to study at home is an impossible luxury - your house or flat may not be big enough, or it may just not be possible to get away from your children. However, for those fortunate to be able to carve out some space, even the kitchen table on a temporary basis, we will find that just as there are some features of training rooms we have considered above, so there are important features of work spaces at home which we should take into account. Many of these features are the same as those covered earlier, but with a different emphasis, whilst some are new:

• *Ownership*: Who does the space belong to - are they going to want it back just when you're in the middle of your work? Having your *own* space means that you can do just what you want in it, arrange things to suit you.

• *Associations*: Does the space have any special or particular associations? E.g. a

Did you know...
what psychologists have found out about practice and skill?

3

One of the few enduring findings of modern psychology is that skilled performance improves with practice. That is to say that repeated attempts at a skilled task result in better performance as measured by fewer errors. (This is good news for those of us still trying to get our counselling skills right!) Although most of the experiments have been done with simple motor skills, e.g. manipulating physical objects, there are, some factors which make the issue of practice and performance a little more complicated, which are worth knowing when it comes to studying counselling.

• Firstly, practice on its own is inadequate; feedback is essential. Acquiring a skill seems to follow a different pattern to learning ideas. This is the difference between knowing *what* to do and knowing *how* to do it (or being able to do it). This is a familiar problem for us all and we recognise this as a stage in acquiring a skill - our brain knows what we should do, but the rest of us hasn't quite got the hang of it yet. This is where *repeated practice with feedback* comes in, it is the key to successful skill acquisition.
• Secondly it appears that the way in which the practice is organised has an important effect upon the outcome. If the practice is lumped together in one big bunch (called massed practice) it takes longer to acquire the skill than if the practice is spread out (called distributed practice). Psychologists measure succes in skilled performance by looking at the types of errors made and it appears that errors seem to disappear in the breaks between bouts of distributed practice, whereas they disappear much more slowly when practice is done in a big lump.

How can we use these findings?
If feedback plays such an important role in learning new skills, we need to give good, constructive feedback to our peers. Feedback which simply says 'wrong', 'wrong', 'wrong' is disheartening at an emotional level and so won't be heard. It is a good idea to have a strategy such as the following: make *three* positive comments, suggest *two* ways of doing things differently and *one* negative comment.

When it comes to practising counselling skills, spread out your practice. That is to say, take breaks, don't squeeze practice into a short space of time, leave enough gaps for your errors to disappear, give your skills time to consolidate between moderate bursts of practice. Don't try to get it perfect too quickly.

bedroom might be associated with sleep or sex, a table in the kitchen or dining room might be associated with social chatting etc. If you are having difficulty concentrating on work, it may be because the space you are trying to work in is associated with another activity. For example, if you use a bedroom for study, try to make it a *dedicated* study space whilst you study - make a space by spreading your books out. Sit in a chair, don't lie on the bed to read.

• *Availability*: Can you use the space whenever you want or is it limited to certain times of the day when no-one else is using it? Many of us will be limited to certain spaces at certain times of the day, we do not have the luxury of a study or personal space. It may help to make a weekly timetable for using the space - that will help you and other members of your family keep the time and the space free for you, and it may help you develop a regular routine if you want to.

• *Suitability*: Does it have the right sort of furniture, etc? Is it quiet enough? You may have to reorganise things a little to make the space suitable for study.

• *Privacy*: If you require privacy in order to work, are you going to get it here? Let others know that you are studying and require privacy, again, a timetable may help here, certain times of the day can become known as your study times.

• *Useability*: Can you do what you like in the room - scatter papers on the floor, stick things on the wall to remind you to this or that?

How important you think these features of personal study space are will depend upon your preferences and needs. It helps to spend a few minutes contemplating your personal requirements for study space at home. Most of us do not do this - we just make assumptions based upon habit. The problem is that our study habits are quite likely to have been formed many years ago when we were studying subjects with very different learning requirements from counselling.

Activity - Study space at home
Do this with a friend or peer from your course to help challenge your habits and contribute new ideas.

• Think about the available space at home.
   • What spaces could you use straight away or adapt for study at home?
• What are your personal needs and preferences when it comes to personal study space at home (use the features listed above)?
   • What arrangements do you need to make on a physical level (moving furniture etc.), and in relationships (asking for undisturbed time) in order to get your needs met?

Time - the last resource

Time is a precious resource to many people and it is easy for them to believe that they don't have enough of it to get all the important things done in their busy lives. Some people, on the other hand, have time to spare. They search for ways to fill time productively and save themselves from boredom. My own experience is that time has a curious elastic property to it. It stretches to fit my necessary tasks with a magical quality, yet I never seem to have enough

Did you know...

4

what psychologists have found out about paying attention?

I have put these *attention* and *perception* panels next to each other because the two processes are linked very closely together. In simple terms, psychologists have been interested in how the nature of the attention we pay to something affects our ability to sense and understand it. Aside from the extremes of this debate (i.e. Does *subliminal perception* [being presented with an image so fast that we are not aware of its presence] have any effect upon behaviour, or even exist?) the results are clear and unequivocal - paying close attention to something improves our ability to make sense of it.

Selective attention

Psychologists have discovered that we have the ability to notice important things going on in the background when we are paying attention to a particular thing. Some things have a greater tendency to distract us than others, such as hearing our name spoken or seeing something intrinsically more interesting (such as bright colours). Once our attention has been distracted, however, it transpires that we have taken in nothing of the material that we were originally attending to. In short, human beings are pretty useless at paying attention to more than one thing at a time.

Paying attention and Attentional inertia

Attentional inertia is the phenomenon of something holding our attention, not because we are interested in it, but because our attention is held in a trance-like state. Ominously, researchers (Anderson and others 1979) studied the way children watch television and concluded that after watching TV for a relatively short while (10 minutes), it is easier to watch the screen than to look away. This finding is in accord with others which demonstrate that we cannot pay attention for long periods of time. After about 20 minutes, we stop paying attention. We would be wrong to call this 'boredom.' Humans pay more attention to varied, changing stimuli and tasks, especially those which require active involvement.

How can we use these findings

Being distracted from our study is bad news. Too many other things going on around us, however much we may kid ourselves, really will mean that were not taking anything in. Also, whenever we are in class it is better to have the styles of input varied with tasks that involve activities to ensure we continue to pay close attention and do not suffer from attentional inertia, listening in a trance-like state to the tutors voice...

and always feel under pressure. I know that my problem is organisation, or as they say in some books 'time management', and I know I am not alone! Whilst for the majority of people it may be a question of organising time, I also know that some factors beyond our choice or control limit the amount of useable time we have available. From work commitments to childcare, life will insist on filling each day with genuinely important things to do that get put higher up our list of priorities than studying.

Organising your study time
Even if our time is truly limited by childcare, work and other responsibilities, we can usually nibble away at the margins to create enough time for studying. Increasing our self awareness is always a good way to start, so the first step in organising our time is to find out how we use time in a typical week. The chart below is a blank weekly timetable. It might seem to you that a timetable is an unacceptable way of over-structuring your time. However, monitoring the way we spend time helps us to see the natural rhythms in our lives (sleeping, waking, eating, travelling, leisure, etc.) and helps us establish some new rhythms built around learning counselling (*weekly* timetable, *term* dates, *annual* assessments etc.) I suggest you make a copy and fill it in for one week using the following categories of activity (you can adjust the times to fit your typical day - i.e. starting and finishing earlier or later):

		a.m.			<	Time	>	p.m.								
	7	8	9	10	11	12	1	2	3	4	5	6	7	8	9	10
S U N																
M O N																
T U E																
W E D																
T H U																
F R I																
S A T																

• *Essential:* Sleep, eating, travel, family chores, etc. (Be careful to make sure that, for example, meal times are reasonable, rather than two-hour social occasions.)

• *Leisure:* This should speak for itself, and will include reading the newspapers, and watching the TV, as well as going out for the evening or to a football match.

• *Study:* Be honest with the timings. Don't count time spent gazing into space with a book open in front of you. That's not study. However, make a reasonable allowance for 'thinking time' or personal contemplation, both of which are creditable activities for a counselling trainee.

This task may not have been easy either on a practical level (life is messy and the elements just will not be easily separated into nice chunks), or on an emotional level (you may not like having your life categorised and boxed off in this way). This raises an important issue in study skills. Do not feel *forced* to accept the imposition of order on your personal chaos. If you discover that you thrive on chaos and *do not want to and will not* think in an organised or strategic way about study and time, then don't. If you need to 'go with the flow', go with it. You can always return to this activity if you ever feel the need to. At least by attempting this exercise thus far, you will have discovered something about how you prefer to structure your life - if you didn't know it already.

Using time effectively

This exercise doesn't tell us exactly how we typically use time for two reasons. Firstly the very act of measuring something changes it, so you will have changed your behaviour slightly. Secondly, you will not have timed yourself absolutely accurately - a bit like not counting the calories accurately when you're on a diet.) Still, it should be good enough to get a rough base line from which to plan your use of time.

•The next task is to get a total for each category of activity; essential, leisure and study. You may well have a target number of study hours to find in a week. This could be a figure suggested or recommended by the course or one that you have worked out for yourself, knowing your own capabilities.

•Next shade in or highlight the different categories of time with a different colour, e.g. blue for essential, red for leisure, etc. The aim of this whole exercise is not to just follow natural patterns of time or let your usual routine continue to dominate your week. We are going to take an *active* approach to shaping your week strategically so that you have time for each activity.

Now take a look at the week and the totals and ask yourself the following questions:

• Do I have a target number of study hours?
If not, ask your course tutor for a suggestion. Does it sound reasonable to you, or might you need more time because you've not been used to studying for a few years?

• Am I hitting this target?
If you are undershooting your target, first look critically at your week and figure out if there are any 'grey areas' where the leisure or essential activities are more flexible. See if you can reasonably allocate more time to study. Don't set any arrangements in stone yet - wait until you have gone through all of these questions and even then, stay flexible.

• What does the pattern of activities look like?

Are they spread evenly around the week or is the study bunched up in a solid block over one day?

Effective study needs different chunks of time for different activities:

- *Half an hour snatched here and there will do for reading through your notes or an essay plan.*
- *Whereas you need to break from the atmospheres and activities around you, change gear and create the right atmosphere for preparing for an essay or reading and understanding new material.*
- Have you allowed yourself decent breaks?

Do not work for hours on end without a break. Your ability to concentrate and therefore your effectiveness will suffer after around one hour. Give yourself 10 minutes in every hour, unless you are 'on a roll' and know that to stop will make more work. After a while you will train yourself to work in these blocks of time.

Making decisions about using time

Now you can begin to plan strategically for study. You will need a diary or calendar in front of you to take an overview of the year ahead. Mark in when assignments are due and make a note of the approximate amount of time required to complete each one. Next, with a few copies of the blank weekly timetable, look ahead to the study tasks that are coming up in the next three or four weeks. Shade in a timetable of 'essential', 'study', and 'leisure' times. (Note the order here - essential first, followed by study.) Let your leisure fit in around study. Give yourself regular breaks. Put in some time for thinking and reflection, and allow some study time for further *planning*.

Deciding how to use your available study time can be more difficult than it seems. I know from my own experience that I can spend a lot of time 'planning' (i.e. putting off the dreadful moment when I must actually get down to some real work!) The following questions are begging for direct, sensible answers:

- How should I prioritise the various tasks I have to achieve?
- How much work should I try to do in two hours?
- How much reading time should I allocate for an essay?

The trouble with these questions, and the whole planning approach to study, is that we could be tricked into believing that study can be *completely* compartmentalised and divided into neat achievable tasks, each one time limited and discrete. I suppose that if you are a fan of solution-focused time-limited therapy then you will find this planning rewarding. As a person-centred counsellor, however, I do not like to cleanse chaos from my life completely. I like the creativity that seems to come at those chaotic and unstructured moments. I find it difficult to timetable inspiration in to my week! I have, though, benefitted from planning and organisation of my time in ways that follow me and my patterns, ways that suit *me* best. This section is intended to offer a framework, a possible way of planning which you may find helpful, you may reject but feel inspired to devise your own, or you may think it is not for you at all. Remember, though, that however unstructured you may wish to be, there *will* be deadlines and criteria to meet on courses, and however tightly you may wish to tie down your planning, life has a way of messing it up.

Model Answer 1: *Client hours log and Client notes*

The extracts below are included to show firstly how simple a client log is, and secondly a couple of ways of keeping client notes; one where the emphasis is on the client, the other where the emphasis is on the counsellor. Neither is the 'right way', you may have to keep notes of a particular style, but will be able to keep your own personal notes in any way you wish.

Client hours log

Date	Client Identifier	Time	Session No.	Duration	Notes
12/10/94	A	3pm	3	50 mins	Nothing to report.
	B	4pm	11	40 mins	Phoned to say he'd be late.
19/9/94	A	3pm	4	DNA	No message, waited full hour.
	B	4pm	12	50 mins	B on holiday next week - no sess
	C	6pm	1	50 mins	Contract sorted, review 24/10

Client Notes

Client: *P.S.*   Counsellor: *A.N.Other*

Session No.	Date	Notes
12	12/9/94	*Started cheerful but soon got onto the theme of loss. Still not able to really express feelings of sadness and anger about his father's death, but talks a lot about them. Seems to still be in denial and can't move to the next stage of grieving. Has dreams about his father and is upset by them but soon puts it all away. He must express these feelings if he is to move on in this process. Perhaps I will confront him with his lack of expression of grief next session. Review due in two weeks time.*
13	19/9/94	*I felt really good going into this session. I had been able to really clear my mind and prepare for meeting PS. He seemed tired as he came in, but it soon went as he got under way. I felt really warm towards him today, not at all frustrated as I had done last week. I was really able to be present and I felt a real connection. What made the difference I wonder? I must take this to supervision. Is it something he's doing or something in me? I felt a twinge of discomfort later in the session when he was talking about his boyfriend - he really sounds like a heartless bastard. I didn't get drawn into third-party stuff though, and was able to listen well after I acknowledged the discomfort.*

These notes emphasise the client and the c'sellors view of them

These notes emphasise the c'sellor and their experience of themselves in the session

Hints and Tips 3

1. There are three domains which affect learning, inside you, your relationships with others and the external, physical world. Take time to consider the effect each one has upon your learning.

2. Find out about yourself - explore and identify your personal learning style and preferences:
   • Think of something you're good at and try to remember how you learned it.
   • Think of a teacher, friend or relative you liked and helped you learn a new skill or some information.
   • The answers to these questions will give you some clues about your personal learning style and the way you prefer to learn. Keep these in mind as you progress through your course.

3. Do not forget that you learn about, in, and through, relationships on counselling courses. Relationships with others are another key to successful learning: Your peers, your clients, your tutors, your family, your friends, your supervisor.
   • How do you rate yourself at:
      a) being aware of these relationships,
      b) maintaining these relationships,
      c) exploiting the full learning possibilities in these relationships?

4. Organising your studies is central to success:
   • Make a timetable of the year to see how the burden of work distributes itself.
   • Complete the timetable on page 55 and adjust your working pattern if necessary.
   • Keep your friends and family fully informed - you will need their help and support.
   • Make sure those around you know that you will need time and space in which to study undisturbed.

5. Become a listmaker if you are not one already. Make your goals short and specific, review lists regularly and make full use of tutorials to review your progress - listen to what tutors have to say and check with peers.

6. Build variety into your studies and your weekly timetable in general, do not ignore your friends or drop them for the duration of the course.

7. Manage your study spaces at college and at home. If possible make a separate space as special study space. Match the space to the task - don't fall victim to old associations between places and activities, i.e. avoid trying to study in a place that you associate with social chatting or sleep (don't read books lying on your bed.) If in doubt, try it out.

Skills and Techniques for Effective Study

4

1. Note making

The palest ink is better than the sharpest memory.
Chinese Proverb

Most counselling courses are based around group work and the personal experience and input of the participants, but some of the input from your tutors will be in the form of lectures, or you may even have the opportunity to listen to a visiting speaker giving a lecture on some topic relevant to counselling. Even though the majority of your learning will not be from formal lectures don't be tempted to think that note making therefore will not be useful for you, it will, but perhaps in a different form. Note making is another way of *interacting* with the material you're studying so it is a technique to be used with books, journals, radio and TV broadcasts as well as lectures, tutorials and group discussions. Perhaps you'll even find some things worth noting down arising from informal discussions over coffee or a pint.

Just as with reading skills, an emphasis can be placed on the *function* of note making and the *type* of notes. The function of note making in any given situation and the type of material you are making notes from, determine the range of activities which are generally included under the term 'note making'. Also notice two further points:

- that the title reads 'note making' not 'notes', indicating that the *activity* is as important as

the content of the end product and secondly,

- I have called it note *making* not note *taking* to emphasise the points made above, i.e. that in lectures we may call it note *taking*, since we may try to write word for word, or in rare cases someone might even *dictate* a short passage to us. Note *making* on the other hand is a creative activity. You are in interaction with the material.

Type of Material

There are two broad categories of material from which it is useful to take notes: written material and spoken material:

(1) Making notes from **written material** begins with following the *Preview Checklist* described in the section on 'Strategies for reading' on p.65. Now skim through the material and make a note of those pages and parts of pages which are relevant to your purpose. It's a good idea to mark the book by making a vertical line in the margin in pencil next to the lines that make a particularly important point. College and Public Libraries are quite rightly not keen on this kind of defacing of books, but you could do it to material that belongs to you and erase the marks should you wish to sell it later. Distinguish between quotes from the book and your own notes. It's always best to use your own words whenever possible as this forces you to think about the material.

Your aim should be to:
- condense the material,
- maintain the essential meaning of the material,
- cross-refer it to other notes and work.
- relate it to the reason you are making the notes (e.g. an essay or forthcoming exam).
- to demonstrate to yourself that you understand because you can put the information in your own words - rather like the skill of reflection in a counselling session.

2)   The main form of **spoken material** from which students take notes is the lecture. The trouble with lectures (and lecturers) is that no two are the same in the demands that they make on the student. Some lecturers expect the student to be totally self-sufficient. They give no handouts and few references. Others give handouts summarising the main points of the lecture, references to further reading and use the lecture as a vehicle for increasing understanding as well as imparting information. You must first decide what sort of lecture you are in, then your task will become easier. There's not much point in writing notes that summarise the main points if you're going to be given a handout which does this for you.

Notes taken from lectures range all the way from the verbatim account (if you're good at shorthand) to the barest of outlines. The amount you need to take will depend upon:
- the content of the lecture (lectures which have a heavy 'factual' content may require more notes),
- how familiar you are with the material,
- whether there are alternative sources of the information, e.g. textbooks.

It is, generally speaking, a mistake to take down every word uttered by the lecturer. Lectures include a great deal of redundant material. This 'rubbish' is in the form of repetition, multiple examples, re-emphasis, jokes, anecdotes, etc. Those students who fill page after page with copious notes do so as a kind of safety net because they often cannot understand the lecture enough to tell the difference between the *useful* and the *useless* material. You need time to think about the material that is being presented to you in a lecture, so don't spend all your time feverishly writing things down. Some general hints are:
- Take down as much as you need to understand the lecture.
- Pay attention to the accuracy of tables, charts and diagrams.
- Use abbreviations wherever possible.
- Leave plenty of space between points so that you can go back to expand upon a point made earlier.
- Re-write your lecture notes at the earliest possible time, if possible incorporating notes taken from textbooks.

If you are returning to study after a number of years 'lay off' it would probably help if you could practise your note making skills before you actually get into the lecture situation. One way of doing this is to take notes from radio programmes (Open University programmes are particularly good, pick one or two from a relevant course). You could also try making notes on the story lines in your favourite soap opera, if you have one, or anything else on TV, to help you engage fully in the content and process of what is happening and to practise making notes at speed, as it happens, and without the benefit of a rewind button.

Functions of notes

Regardless of the type of material, the most important questions to ask yourself are 'Why am I making these notes?' and 'What am I going to use them for?' You must make your notes fit your needs; *general* notes rarely if ever suit *specific* needs. Imagine two students sitting in the same lecture on work motivation. One has to write an essay evaluating various theoretical approaches while the other has to answer a multiple-choice test on the subject thirty minutes after the end of the lecture. Their notes would be different in both content and appearance. Specific needs require specific types of notes, so we must pay attention to the *function* that we expect the notes to fulfil.

Here is a list of some of the functions of note making. Add any which particularly apply to your course of study:

• Making notes to help you pay attention and concentrate. It's a good idea to take notes for no other reason than to stop you drifting off into daydreams. Remember, you learn little or nothing if you are not paying attention. This relates as much to written material as lectures

• Making notes to help you gain a deeper understanding of a subject. This function is likely to be slightly different for different types of material; a transcript of a counselling session or a tape of the 'real' thing will require different notes than, for example, a student's

presentation of a theory of personality that is new to you.

• Making notes to summarise the main points. Remember some lecturers give handouts and some books have chapter summaries.

• Making notes to record detailed facts about events, actions or information. Check the accuracy of your record.

• Making notes to help with a specific assignment, e.g. an essay. Select the information from the book or lecture in a consistent and systematic way, don't write *everything* down.

Making Notes

It's best to write notes on one side of A4 paper (if you can afford it and don't mind the apparent waste of paper). Then you can develop ideas and add to the notes on the other side of the page at a later date or when you are reviewing what you have written soon after the notes were taken. If the notes are on one side of paper they can be cut up into points and shuffled around into topics and connections can be made with notes from other pieces of paper.

Write notes as pictorially as possible. Break them down under large headings and sub-headings and illustrate with diagrams or doodles if these help. Divide points up with numbers for example and different coloured pens may help with memory and organisation.

Methods of making notes

Sprays or webs

Use plenty of space. From a lecture on 'Theories of Personality' a spray would be done in two parts like this:

1) Put down the main ideas in any order, e.g.

Theories of Personality

Freud   *Behaviourism*
              Jung
Carl Rogers   *TA*
              parent/child   *id*
Gestalt   *Fritz Perls* *self concept*

2) Join related items together with lines and arrows at a later time as part of your reviewing your notes or during the lecture if you have enough time.

Flow diagram

Good for remembering, easy to see workings, quicker to draw than to write. Use plenty of space. During a lecture part of it may have a logical sequential structure which can be represented by writing the topic in a box and then linking it to other boxes with arrows to show the flow and development of the idea. (If X happens then Y follows from it.)

Short notes

Taken from talks that you are familiar with, or from discussions or chats that require you to be participating where time for writing very is limited. Just jot down single words, phrases, sentences, shorthand and abbreviated words that will give you a flavour of the material.

Long notes

Taken from lectures where the material is completely new to you and where you are not required to participate. From books where you have the time to read and make detailed notes for reproduction in an essay. Underline/circle key words/phrases. Structure under headings and with different colours. Leave space to add ideas that occur later. Write a summary in a few sentences as a way of checking your understanding and to make revision easier. Parts of the lecture that you find particularly complicated you may even need to write down verbatim.

Note: Always go back to your notes soon after making them to add ideas that have occurred to you later and to check that you still understand them - fill in any gaps that come to your attention.

Storing Notes

Filing/storing your notes is important. If I wasn't so disorganised myself, I would worry that this bit is just too obvious and patronising, but so many of us fail to do the blindingly obvious that it won't hurt to be reminded. Notes are best stored in a loose-leaf ring binder so that they can be arranged in a logical order or put with other notes on the same topic as they arise. It's no good making notes if once you have put them away you can't find them again. Keep similar topics together e.g.

- Skills practice notes inc. tapes and transcriptions
- Theory
  - Person-Centred
  - Behavioural
  - TA
  - Gestalt etc.

- Supervision
    - a diary of what you learned
    - concerns for next meeting
- Assignments
    - Personal journal
    - Book reviews
    - Essays
- Course documentation
- Book lists
- Reading done, useful books reference, reading log etc.

Making notes may not be the prime skill required on your counselling course, and filing those that you do make may seem like a chore, but notes made and not stored in a logical order are notes lost. Unless you can find them and use them you have more-or-less wasted your time making them.

2. Strategies for reading

If asked how they would like their reading improved, most people would say that they would wish *to read faster*. Will this in fact help them to study more successfully?

In 1959 William Perry reported on the reading skills of members of a reading improvement course at Harvard University. The course consisted of 1,500 of the 'finest freshmen readers in the country'. On all the conventional reading tests, these students were scoring highly; they were fast readers with good vocabularies. Perry gave them a simple task:

twenty minutes to read a chapter on Anglo-Saxon England and then to write a short statement saying what the chapter was all about.

Less than 1 per cent could give a good account of the chapter's contents. What went wrong? They all tried to read the chapter word for word from beginning to end. Perry had deliberately given them a chapter that was too long to read in this manner in the time allowed, but at the end of the chapter was a summary which could be read in ten minutes or so. If only they had skimmed through the chapter first to see how it was laid out! Perry concluded, 'As a demonstration of obedient purposelessness in the reading of 99 per cent of freshmen, we found this impressive.' Tutors are *not* impressed by purposeless obedience!

It has been estimated that the average reading speed in this country for everyday material is around 200 words per minute, with comprehension around 50 per cent. This is bad news for serious students! We need to aim for a reading speed of around double the average *and* increase comprehension if we are to make studying more effective. Here are some techniques which should increase your reading speed.

The first thing to do is to find out how fast you can already read. This can be measured very roughly by reading for five minutes, counting the number of words you've read and dividing by five. This will give you your reading speed in words per minute. Remember, the target speed is 400 wpm. Most people read slowly because they commit errors in reading skills.

There are several possible reasons for poor reading speed:

(1) Too many fixations
(2) Vocalisation and sub vocalisation
(3) Regression
(4) Failure to realise the purpose for reading.
(5) Poor vocabulary.
(6) Lack of concentration.
(7) Inappropriate reading environment.

Getting rid of these 'bad habits' and practising reading quicker will have a dramatic effect on your reading speed, and your understanding of what you have read.

1 Fixations

As we read, our eyes do not scan across each line of print smoothly, they jump across in a series of jerky movements, stopping a number of times on each line. Each time your eyes stop in this way is called a *fixation*. Most people make far more fixations on each line than is really necessary to read the material. The first technique is to cut down on the number of fixations.

Try reading this first block below.

Rogers' views   have been   incorporated into our culture   in many   ways: not   only do psychologists   talk about   being person or client   centred, but   education now talks about   being student   centred

In this block you are encouraged by the layout to 'take in' two words with each fixation.

Now try reading the second block below.

and even industry   and commerce want to be 'customer-   centred'! Many in the 1980s and   90s are attracted   to the basic humanity of his   approach. One favourite criticism of his   approach made by behaviourists is that   the Person-Centred Approach only works   because when Rogers is understanding, genuine   and warm towards his clients he   is doing nothing   more than teaching them to do   the same and   so they become understanding, genuine and   warm themselves.

Now the number of words taken in with each fixation is three. You can practise increasing your *word span* by taking an old book and making marks in pencil every three or four words and training yourself to fixate on the marks for a second or two then moving on to the next mark. When you are competent at three or four words increase to five then to six words.

2 Vocalisation

Vocalisation is the tendency to move your lips or even actually speak the words as you are reading them. This is a bad habit because we can actually read much faster than we can speak! Almost as bad is the tendency to speak the words silently under your breath without moving your lips. This is called sub-vocalisation. It is not surprising that people read in this way since this is how we all learned to read in the first place, but there really need be no connection between speaking and reading for adults. To help get rid of vocalisation you must let your eyes move smoothly across the line of text using the technique of few fixations outlined above. This way you will lose the tendency to read individual words (and therefore *speak* them as you go along), and be able to look at *groups* of words. You will be able to concentrate on the *meaning* of the groups of words rather then the individual words.

You could get a friend to help you with these first two techniques; simply sit facing your friend holding a book up between you. Your friend must be able to see your eyes and mouth as you read. They can then see whether you make many or few fixations *and* whether you have a tendency to vocalise. At the same time they can also give you good feedback on whether you commit the third error in reading, namely that of *regression.*

3 Regression
Regression is simply the tendency to read the same word or group of words twice. You re-read the phrase for no good reason other than bad habit. Of course regression can be a symptom of things other than bad reading habits; over-eagerness, excited scanning of the material or even sheer loss of concentration.

As a first step to help with the problem of regression you must read a passage and *be aware* of your regressions *and why you commit them*. If there is a good reason (such as the ones mentioned above) then you must concentrate more keenly on your reading. If there seems to be no good reason to re-read the words, you must tackle the problem as follows:
- Read for meaning, pay less attention to individual words.
- Re-train your eyes by using your hand as a guide. This may make you feel as though you're back at primary school, but it really

does work. Move your hand at a comfortable speed underneath the line of text. Move smoothly at a constant speed making no pauses, quickly returning to the beginning of the next line.

4 Purpose
Before you read anything, ask yourself 'Why am I reading this?' and 'How well do I need to understand and remember this material?' If you are not sure why you are reading any book, or what you are wanting to do with the learning you have gained from the material your reading will be less effective, if not totally fruitless. An appropriate reading speed will be determined by the complexity of the material and your familiarity with the subject. The layout of the text will make a great deal of difference to your way of tackling it; if the text is very dense with a small type-face is it much more difficult to approach than text that is well spaced and offering a variety of formats. It is no accident that this book is laid out the way it is. (Do you find it easy to read? Please let us know if you don't).

5 Vocabulary
If the subject is completely new to you, you may not be familiar with the jargon that goes with it. Also if your vocabulary doesn't include the words used in the text you will continually be stopping to use a dictionary. This may be frustrating but is worthwhile as your need to do so will diminish in time.

6 Concentration
If you have other things on your mind, are feeling ill or under pressure then your concentration will suffer and therefore so will your reading. Try

wherever possible to set aside a space in your head if you have some heavy reading to do.

7 Environment

For some people sitting in the family room while the children are enthusiastically playing video games will not help your reading but for others being locked away in a room free from interruptions or 'family contamination' will not help either so make sure you find a place that is conducive for reading.

Different reading purposes

There are several reasons why we might read a book or article. Each reason has a different purpose behind it. The following list of purposes will help you identify the type of reading skills you will need.

(1) You are just going into a tutorial on a book which you haven't yet read. You have three minutes to check out what it's about before the tutorial starts. You will *skim* through this book looking for hints like chapter headings and sub-headings, index and summaries.

(2) You have been given a book to review and have two weeks to write a 150 word piece. You will be reading this book *critically*, trying to ascertain its worth. You may have to read the whole book before you can form an opinion - *detailed reading*, or you may be able to make a judgement fairly quickly by *reading for information*.

(3) You have broken your leg, and your friends bring you an interesting looking novel to read, this you will read this purely for *enjoyment* and any pace that suits you and in any way, (I had a friend who always read the end of the book first!)

(4) You have an essay to write and you have assembled a few books which look from their titles as though they might be useful.

(5) You may, if you are wanting to learn more about how writers write so that you can improve your own writing skills, read a book not for its content, but for its structure and the style of writing, this is *analytical reading*.

(6) You have a train timetable, to find the specific train you are looking for you will be *reading for information*.

(7) You have a particular need to find a specific piece of information that is located on a page you have been 'sent to' by the index. In order to find that information you will let your eyes run over the page searching for the particular words you want - this is *scanning* and can save a huge amount of time.

How to tackle a book for study

Reading for entertainment should be familiar to everyone and is probably the only occasion when we would read a book by opening at page one reading word for word from cover to cover. In all other cases the first step should be *previewing the material to be read*. There is usually no need to read all of every book - this one included. It is most efficient to *read only what is relevant to you*
.

When buying a book, most people try to get the 'feel' of it by quickly flicking through the pages, reading the cover notes, looking at a few pictures or diagrams, going through the table of contents etc. This is more or less what I mean by *previewing* the material, it helps you find out which bits of the material will be useful to you without you wasting time actually *reading* it all. Instead of a haphazard process I suggest you follow a checklist such as the one below.

Preview Checklist.

Read the book in this order.

(1) *The Title*. This tells you the general subject area (is it appropriate?). A subtitle will also give you clues. Make a note of the title, the author(s), the publisher(s), the publication date.

(2) *Author*. How qualified and experienced is the author? Look for information about them - usually at the front or back of the book; this may also include a list of their other publications which can help you decide if they will have anything useful to say on the topic you are researching.

(3) *Publisher*. Are they noted for the quality counselling books they publish?

(4) *Date of publication*. The back of the title page will tell you when and where the book was first published, how many reprints it's had (the more there are the more popular the book is and therefore it may be more useful for you). It will also tell you if the book is a new edition meaning that it will have been revised since it was first written - always try to get the latest editions so you can benefit from any new material.

(5) *The cover notes or blurb*. These tell you the level at which the book is pitched (Introductory course, certificate, diploma or MA) and the style of coverage given to the subject.

(6) *Table of Contents*. Do the contents relate to your reason for reading the book? Can you pick out headings which you recognise and those which you think may be useful? *Write down* the list of contents.

(7) *Introduction/Preface*. This should tell you the scope and purpose of the book and how the book should be used to get the best out of it.

(8) *Index*. What does the index tell you about the contents of the book. Are there many names and dates or does the book seem to concentrate on concepts? Does the book suit your purpose?

(9) *Conclusion*. Unlike a novel it is not a 'sin' to read the end first. The conclusion can save you a lot of time. Alternatively the opening or closing paragraphs of each chapter will give you some idea of the contents.

(10) *Bibliography/References* This is the list of publications the author has consulted or quoted from. The dates of publication will give you an idea of how up-to-date the author's work is.

Having done this you will have a fair idea what the book is about without reading a word of the text! Keep a file of all the titles, authors, publishers and contents of the books you have previewed in this way. It will be invaluable when planning essays and assignments.

The next stage is to approach the text but not necessarily at page one.

First using your preview, select the part you are interested in, the part that suits your purpose. (Obviously this doesn't apply if you need to read the whole book.)

Second With a pen and paper at the ready in case you want to make comments, *skim* over the whole piece noting the structure of the material, subheadings, tables, diagrams, overviews and summaries.

Third Read the overviews and summaries (if there are any) making notes on the central ideas that the author is trying to convey.

Fourth Read the text. Again make sure you have a pen and paper handy to jot down notes as you go along, remembering to make reference to page numbers as you go if that will help you locate material for future reference.

Now, having read the book do you understand the material? Can you remember it? Now is the time to *review* what you have just read. Think back over the text and without looking at the pages, using you own words, see if you can describe the main ideas expressed in the material. Again it is better if you put pen to paper at this point, because as you become more *actively involved* in the material, the more you will learn and remember from what you have just read.

This *progressive elaboration* of the material means that you can read to the depth that suits your purpose - from last minute cramming before a tutorial to reading an entire book to gain deep understanding.

Abbreviations used in footnotes

ibid in the same book as noted in the last footnote
op. cit. in the book already mentioned
ff. and the following pages
pp. pages
cf. compare

3. Getting the most out of libraries

Many people are intimidated by libraries until they become familiar with them. This is mainly because they don't understand how libraries work, so it's necessary to look at the services offered by libraries and the types of classification system they use for easy storage and retrieval of books and other materials.

Getting to know the library that you are going to use most frequently is the best starting point, once you have mastered that then others are organised on much the same lines with variations of layout and contents. Start by trying the activity below.

Perhaps you're one of the many people who goes to pieces in a library and are afraid of asking for assistance in case you appear foolish. Perhaps you're tempted to sit at home doing nothing just to avoid libraries, or, when you're forced to use one, wandering round lost until in frustration you go home with your fears confirmed. If you really are lost in or scared of libraries, then the librarian will be only too pleased to help. Often colleges employ a *tutor librarian* whose job it is to teach people about the library, how it works and how to get the best out of it. Remember libraries are there to help you and you have every right to make them work to capacity for you.

Libraries are simple to understand and everyone can learn to use them effectively in a short space of time.

Activity - knowing your library

• *What are the opening times of your local, or your College Library?*
• *Is there a leaflet available describing the library facilities? Have you got one?*
• *What classification system does your library use?*
• *What catalogue medium is used? Card, microfilm, microfiche, CD Rom or a mixture?*
• *Is there a separate catalogue for journals and periodicals? What journals relevant to your course does the library take?*
• *How many books are you allowed to borrow at any one time and for how long? What are the penalties for not returning book on time?*
• *Can you reserve books already out on loan?*
• *Is the library a place you could work in? For example does it have large tables or small personal cubicles to suit your requirements? Does it have the right atmosphere - not too formal, not too relaxed?*

All you have to do is get familiar with them. Take your time, wander around getting the feel of the place, look in all the nooks and crannies. Most of all seek out the librarian or assistant librarians; your tutors should be able to tell you which ones are particularly used to dealing with counselling queries. If you are not training at a college or university with its own library ask your tutors which of your local libraries will be of most use and start the 'getting to know it' process there.

There are several ways of familiarising yourself with your library and it's always best to make time spent in the library productive which means making your task of learning about the library relevant to *your* course. A good first step is to seek the advice of your tutor-librarian. If your library doesn't have such a person and the librarian is unable to help, here are a few things to do which you can tailor to the requirements and content of your particular course.

• Get hold of a copy of the recommended reading list for your course. (If there isn't one, ask your tutor for the titles and authors of half a dozen useful books.) Then find out how many of the titles the library has in the catalogue. Locate the position on the shelves and see how many are currently available.
• Make a list of the subject areas that your course covers, then locate these in the library. Note that one topic area may have sub-topics located in different places in the library.

Familiarise yourself with these locations.

• A library contains a variety of publications. It will be a good idea to find out whether the library takes journals relevant to your course, and locate them. Now find out what other resources the library has that may be of relevance to you, reference books, audio cassettes, magazines etc.

• Not all of the material available in the library is kept on display, so check with the librarian on what is kept in special rooms.

• Have a look in the reference section at the almanacs and yearbooks. These can be an invaluable source of information, addresses and statistics.

Now, although there are some slight differences between libraries (public lending libraries contain different sorts of books from university or college libraries), their organisation is often very similar. The minor differences that do exist can be quickly sorted out by asking the librarian and/or picking up a leaflet describing the library facilities, opening times etc. This should help you realise that libraries contain much more than just 'books'.

 Get to know the library staff; it's their job, and their pleasure, to help students use the library they work so hard to build and maintain. They have nothing invested in keeping books on shelves. In order to avoid wasting time getting lost in disorganised searching the next thing you have to do is to learn the method of finding particular books.

Finding material in a library
The library catalogue is the list that will tell you not only whether your library has a particular book, but also where it's kept in the library. There are two types of catalogue in each library: the *classified catalogue* and the *alphabetical catalogue*. The alphabetical catalogue lists the *author* and *subject headings* of the books in alphabetical order and it is this catalogue that most people learn to use with little problem. However, it gives you the location of the book in terms of the *classification system* (a series of numbers or letters given to each subject for identification and location purposes).

A common question is, *'How do the numbers tell you where the book is in the library?'* The books are arranged in the library in the same order as in the classified catalogue, usually starting near the library entrance and proceeding in a clockwise direction. In any event the first thing you should do when entering the library is look at the floor plan which will give you the layout with the classification numbers. Also you should find the classification numbers actually on the shelves perhaps at the end nearest a gangway, as well as some broad subject headings.

What to do if...
• *You want to find a book but only know the author.* Look up the surname in the author catalogue or microfiche to find the classification number which tells you where the book is shelved - look on the floor plan for where the books with this number are located. In some libraries these may be card indexes in large wooden trays, they may also be on microfiche, computer print-out or computer screen.
• *You want to find a book but only know its title.*

If the book is still in print find the title in *British Books in Print*, you may need to access the latest update if the book has only just been published. If the book is likely to be out of print you may have to ask the library staff to help you find the author.

• *If the library has the book but you can't find it.* If the book you want is out with another reader it is usually possible to reserve the book for a small fee. This may mean that you will have to wait several weeks so make sure you plan well ahead if you can. It may also be stored elsewhere in the *Reference Section* for example or if it is a very popular book it may be in a *Short Loan* collection kept behind the counter. The catalogue should tell you this.

• *If the library doesn't have the book you want.* You can ask one of the library staff to get it for you. This will usually mean filling out a form and waiting - often several weeks again so be prepared - for it either to be purchased or ordered through the *Inter Library Loan System*. Tell the librarian if you have a deadline to meet, it may not be possible to get the book in time.

Classification summary

Subject index This lists alphabetically hundreds of subjects, and gives the library code (classification number, very often libraries are classified according to the Dewey System) for each. In other words it tells you where to look in the library but it doesn't list the books.

Author index Every book in the library is arranged here in alphabetical order by author's surnames. This also includes editors and name of committees which have produced reports.

Classified catalogue All the books in the library are recorded here in numerical order according to their classification number. To use this catalogue you have first to find out from the subject index the number for the subjects you are interested in.

4. Exam preparation

Most counselling courses do not have examinations, but some do, (see p.86 & 87 for rationale) so if this applies to you we hope to help you make the most of what you know, so that an exam becomes a satisfying rather than a frustrating experience.

A well prepared student has nothing to fear from an examination. Preparation for the few hours in the exam room is crucial and to prepare inefficiently is to waste your months of hard work that have gone before. Many students believe that revision means sitting down reading passively through books and notes over and over again until some of it sticks. Those who follow this method of exam preparation are destined to feel as though they've not quite done themselves justice.

Exam preparation can be divided into three distinct periods: *Well before the exam*
                  Before the exam
                  During the exam

Well before the exam

During the months before the exam - in fact since the

beginning of the course - you can be preparing for the exam by keeping good notes from tutorials, by keeping records of what you have read, by learning from the feedback to your essays and tapes. In short, exam preparation begins at the start of the course; the more organised you have been in keeping control and track of, and being engaged in, your learning the easier your exam preparation or revision will be.

But as most people leave revision until the last couple of months before the exam how best can preparation be done in these circumstances? First of all, *be systematic in your revision.* Make a timetable of topics to be studied and allocate a length of time for study depending on their complexity, importance and your familiarity with them. It is probably better to schedule a few topics for each day to save you getting too bored with the same thing over long periods of time, 'A change is as good as a rest'. Leave the final week unplanned to cover any last minute crises of confidence and to leave yourself space to relax to reduce any nerves you may have.

Revision of the material to be studied requires active engagement. As with all your work *be discriminating*, revise those things that are most likely to be needed to answer the questions. This doesn't mean that you should gamble on the questions that are likely to appear, but that you should cover only the essential information for any topic. Again *use your tutor for advice* they should be able to point you in the right direction for revision.

Look at past papers to familiarise yourself with their style and to see the structure of the exam. Make sure you understand the meanings of the key words used in exam questions see p.107 in the section on writing essays. Find out the number of questions you have to answer and whether any of them are compulsory, for instance, will you be required to answer questions from each section? How long is the exam? Are you allowed to take any materials or texts in with you to help during the time?

Before the exam
Either revise last thing before you go to bed at night, working on the idea that you'll have less time to forget material or have a complete break. You decide which you think will enhance your performance the next day - a late night session burning the midnight oil or an evening relaxing to take your mind off the next day.

The night before make sure you have everything you need for the next day's exam - last minute rushes do nothing for the blood pressure and may lead to you being too 'psyched up' and thus reduce your performance in the exam. Some people need to get psyched-up in order to perform well, and a 'helpful' tutor once told me 'If you like to be really keyed-up in order to do well then arrange to 'lose' some essential items just a few minutes before you set out, that should get you high enough! (I do not recommend this method!)

Don't compare amounts of revision with other students before you go in to the exam; there will always be the student who has covered everything back-to-front, inside-out and upside-down. Also don't ask them what they decided to revise; you will only get panicked if you think you have left something out.

During the exam

Try not to look up at other people, the way they are doing things cannot help and it may actually hinder you.

Read the rubric (instructions) carefully to make sure you answer all the questions (you should know this in advance, but don't make assumptions). Read all the questions twice. Don't fall into the trap of seeing a word you know and being so pleased to see it there that you forget to read the question around it assuming you know what it's all about - you may be wrong.

Choose your questions carefully and ruthlessly - do the ones you think you can get most marks on, the ones you know most about, not necessarily the ones you like best. Start with your best question while you are still fresh. Don't be tempted to write a lot on only four out of five questions and hope that you can pull the marks up to compensate for missing out a question. It doesn't work like that; it is better to get slightly lower marks on five questions than scrape a few more marks on only four.

Then set about writing the answers as you would do an essay, see p.105ff. although of course with less time. (Take around one fifth of the time allocated to each question to make a plan.) Don't spend too much time on one question to the detriment of others. Divide the time up and time yourself remembering to allow some time for reading the questions and checking at the end. Marks are generally allocated for specific points not for length. As with writing essays always spend a few minutes writing a plan for your exam answers. It will keep you from wandering off the subject and will demonstrate to the tutor what you intended to put in the whole answer if you don't get time to finish.

Checking your answers is always worthwhile, a quick read-through will spot spelling and grammatical errors. Make sure all rough work and mistakes are clearly crossed through. Your name, group etc. will need to be on the front page; don't forget these, they are small things I know, but all the more easy to miss off.

After the exam. Don't talk to others afterwards about how much they wrote or what they said for each question. It's too late to do anything about it now and lowering your spirits (or theirs) will not help.

5. Widening your vocabulary

There are several good reasons why broadening your vocabulary will be of benefit to you. No matter at which point you begin, your vocabulary can always be extended. Each subject has its own specific words and counselling is no exception.

Extending your vocabulary will:
- Make you feel more confident in any training or social situation.
- Help you to follow complex arguments.
- Enable you to select the shade of meaning you require to help your self-expression either in written or spoken form.
- Develop your ability to reflect back and clarify client's feelings more accurately.
- Allow you to select words which are

appropriate in different contexts and situations, for example at a job interview, meeting a new client or talking to a familiar friend.

• Improve your understanding of a larger, more difficult, range of material, e.g. information from cultures different from your own.

• Increase your reading speed because you won't need to stop over unfamiliar words.

• Help you to avoid repetition in writing and make your writing more interesting.

When setting about developing your vocabulary it is most efficient to learn only the words that you need to know. There would be little point (unless you're just curious) in picking up a dictionary, opening it at 'A' and learning all the words you didn't know. Better by far to start with words that are linked to your course. There will be words that come up in training sessions that you do not know ask the tutor to explain them; often a difficult thing to do because we always assume that everyone else knows the word. There is something particularly threatening about not knowing the meaning of a word that is casually bandied around by others - we wouldn't be so embarrassed to admit that we didn't know of a place someone was talking about and may be happy to ask where it was, but an unfamiliar word carries the possibility of humiliation with it.

A useful thing to do at the beginning of a course or new topic would be to make a collection of words you'd not met before and write your own definitions for them using the information gleaned from class and from a good dictionary.

A thesaurus will help extend your vocabulary in your written work. A thesaurus, unlike a dictionary, will not tell you what a word means but will give you an alternative to a chosen word. (Thesaurus - dictionary definition, 'a collection of synonyms and antonyms'; according to a thesaurus, others words to substitute for the word 'thesaurus' are, 'dictionary, lexicon, encyclopaedia, word finder'.) This will be of obvious benefit to your written work because we all have a few favourite words we stick to and a thesaurus will give you some alternatives and add variety to your written expression. A thesaurus will also help you find different shades of meaning to suit your purpose and can jog your memories if you have a word on the tip of your tongue but can't quite recall it.

The best way to extend your vocabulary is by active listening in your training sessions and informal, social discussions afterwards (you can learn as many new words from your peers as you can from your tutors). The most valuable way of learning anything is by being actively involved in it, by engaging fully in the process and method of the training sessions and by immersing yourself in the subject and philosophy of counselling.

There will be times on your course when you are required to speak alone in presentations or tape reviews for example. Perhaps there may even be peer assessment elements where you will need to give feedback on fellow students' tapes or written assignments. Feeling secure about your use of language will give you confidence because the accuracy and fluency of your communication will be facilitated by a wider vocabulary.

Developing Your Vocabulary - The Area of Feelings

Because some of us may not be used to being very expressive where feelings are concerned, we may not have a very large vocabulary of words which we use to describe feelings. It can be very useful to build up the vocabulary of feelings words we use. This is a brainstorming activity for small groups, but you can start it off yourself and then ask your friends to make contributions. Simply think of all the feeling words you know and write them down. You may find that some of the words are alternatives, or indicating a subtle difference in feeling. You could try to group them together under headings if you find it helpful. Then, start using them more often to help you get some 'colour' and richness into your descriptions of feelings.

Angry	Sad	Happy	Hurt	Afraid
annoyed	unhappy	elated	upset	scared
enraged	gloomy	cheery	broken	hesitant
cross	choked up	glad	suffering	insecure
sulky	sullen	festive	crushed	panicky
irate	flat	merry	tortured	terrified
belligerent	mournful	jubilant	heartbroken	shaky
....	....	....	vulnerable....	tense.......

Words about intimacy	Words about interest	Other feeling words
loving	curious	envious
tender	fascinated	jealous
close	inquisitive	bored
sexual	attentive	bold
in-tune	enthusiastic	proud
seductive	absorbed	excited
....	....	....

Develop your vocabulary in this way in whatever area of language and experience you wish.

Developing the use of imagery

Using imagery is making a comparison between one thing and another so that what is said isn't literally true but the meaning is clear from the comparison. You may think that imagery or the use of metaphorical language was something you left behind in your school English classes, but imagery and metaphor are something we all use as a normal part of everyday speech e.g. 'My hands are as cold as ice,' or, 'He soaks it all up like a sponge,' or, 'She was so excited she floated on air.'

Use of images can be of benefit on counselling courses when talking about feelings. Sometimes it's easier to make a comparison with something else when we are trying to convey our feelings or empathise with those of a 'client'. For example someone might say,

'I want a more developed relationship with my boyfriend that will be more worthwhile rather than these snatched meetings that just leave me wanting more and feeling very unsatisfied. It feels like I'm being expected to eat up the crumbs that drop from his table when what I really need is some nourishment from a full meal. I can't live off crumbs.'

If we want to be experienced as empathic by the 'client' it might help if we can share in their images and metaphors. We can simply reflect these images and metaphors, or we can enter into the client's world more actively and develop their metaphors alongside them.

Some people find this quite difficult. If you have never been interested in reading or been rewarded for having a vivid imagination it may be that you think - and therefore are comfortable in speaking - in very literal terms. If you have difficulty in using imagery, you could try developing this way of thinking about and relating to your (and other people's). Since imagery is most frequently used in our culture in literature and poetry, that might be a good place to start.

Activity - Imagery

• Pay attention to imagery that people use in their speech either on TV or in conversation with you. How and when do you use it?
• Practise using imagery more particularly when conveying to someone else that you are understanding what they are saying and feeling.
• Ask for feedback from colleagues when you have been using it to reflect their feelings; have you expressed their feeling accurately and have you even enhanced their understanding of how they feel by the comparison you made?

Language and oppression

Much has been written about the relationship between language and culture. Counsellors-in-training should be well-versed in the principles of equality of opportunity and anti-oppressive practice. However, in the stress of completing assignments we sometimes overlook the possibility of our language being oppressive.

It is simply a matter of making a conscious decision

to write in a way that does not degrade, diminish, overlook or insult a person, their lifestyle or beliefs. In terms of sexist language this can range from the ways we use *she* and *he* in our writing, to the use of 'man' (as in 'She *manned* the desk' - change to 'She staffed the desk'), or assigning genders to jobs (male nurse).

Racism in language is just as deep-rooted, as Benjamin Zephaniah showed in his poem 'White Comedy' in which he describes being branded a 'white sheep', living off the 'white economy' and beaten by the 'white shirts', but don't worry he says, he will write to complain to the 'Black House'. Lest we fall into the trap that Zephaniah is alerting us to, we could try to avoid phrases like: *Christian name* and *black spot*, etc.

Vocabulary and culture

As counsellors we are committed to developing ways of working in ways which acknowledge and celebrate cultural differences. One of the ways we can show our awareness of different cultural traditions is to develop a vocabulary which encompasses them. There are several ways we can do this:
• By deliberately learning about other cultures and religious traditions.
• By opening up our lives in general to the influence of other cultures.
• By attending cross-cultural social events.
• By attending cross cultural workshops.

Hints and Tips 4

1. **Notes:**
   - Get into the habit of making notes.
   - *Make notes* don't *take notes*. This means you've got to interact with the material
   - Don't just copy - *at least* put the material in your own words.
   - Experiment with different ways of making notes and the layout - what material are you making the notes from; written or spoken? What is the purpose of the notes?
   - Look at the way other people make notes - see if you can improve your note-making.

2. **Reading:**
   - Reading speed is not something you're born with - you can improve you reading speed and the amount of information you take in.
   - Avoid making the typical errors in reading:
     Too many fixations,
     vocalisation and
     regression.
   You will need to get a friend to help you to do the exercises.
   - Different types of material lead to different purposes in reading which in turn lead to different ways of reading.
   - Do not read academic books from cover to cover - follow the plan: preview, select, read, making notes as you go.

3. **Libraries:**
   - Don't be afraid of libraries.
   - Library staff are trained and enthusiastic information facilitators - they want you to use the library and find the material you're after. Build good working relationships with them.
     - Look out for a tutor-librarian, specially trained to help students or a specialist in your area.

4. **Exams:**
   - Before the exam, prepare well in advance. Use your time-management skills to plan your revision. Get hold of specimen and past papers, ask tutors for their advice on what's likely to come up.
   - During the exam, relax, read the instructions carefully, choose your questions carefully - don't rush, plan each answer - this is not time wasted, answer the right number of questions, review your answers.

5. **Vocabulary:**
   - As counsellors we have to try to understand the client on their own terms. This will involve increasing our vocabulary - whatever your background. Become more aware of the words you use.

Assessment and Assignments On Counselling Courses

5

Assessment

Most of us may think that we are used to being assessed in an educational or training environment. However, one or two problems can arise as far as assessment is concerned:

- Assessment can be a painful process. It is nearly always difficult to accept feedback of an evaluative sort and doubly difficult if, as is the case on counselling courses, the feedback also contains some evaluation of what we might consider to be more *personal* qualities.
- It may be quite a few years since we were last at school or college as a student and we may have forgotten just how difficult submitting our work for assessment actually is and what kind of personal, emotional investment it requires.
- Also, we may just be out of date as far as understanding modern assessment methods is concerned. Traditional 'homework' and 'tests' are not a feature of adult education and certainly not popular on counselling courses.
- We may associate assessment with being criticised, put down or marked out as a failure. On the other hand, some of us may associate assessment with always being top of the class and finding academic things very easy. Either way, we may have to revise our views and this may be more difficult than we have bargained for.

- The educational ethos on counselling courses tends to be one where participants are expected to take responsibility for the meeting of assignment deadlines. You will not be chivvied or chased for your work, if you miss a deadline without negotiation you may simply fail the assignment.

Why are counselling courses different?

There is no doubt that counselling courses ask us to present different types of evidence in different ways from, for example, GCSE Maths or a Degree in Psychology. You may, perhaps, be used to writing essays or sitting tests and exams. The majority of counselling courses are training course participants to be practitioners; either counsellors or counselling skills practitioners. It is common for courses that are concerned with practical performance to have some form of practical assessment; for example, trainee chefs are expected to demonstrate that they can cook a range of dishes. In counselling training, this means us showing that we understand, and can demonstrate, the appropriate use of counselling skills. This need to assess practical counselling skills leads to certain types of assignment.

Even when counselling training does require an academic assignment, such as an essay, or in some cases sitting an exam, it is often a requirement that personal experience is integrated into the piece of

work. This can be more difficult than it seems at first sight:
• We may simply be not used to writing about our personal experience in such a way as makes sense to others.
• Some people rebel against academic writing by going too far in the direction of personal experience when given half a chance.
• Properly *integrating* personal experience and academic material is a real skill which may require several attempts and some guidance from tutors before you can get it right.

Another reason why counselling courses are different is that generally speaking, courses try to have an educational method (this includes assessment) that is in harmony or congruent with the theoretical approach of the course in particular (Person-Centred, Psychodynamic, Integrative, etc.) and counselling in general. This often comes out in the style of assessment, such as whether there is much peer-evaluation (where course participants evaluate each other) or self-evaluation (where course participants are asked to evaluate themselves).

Many counselling trainers take the view that since self awareness is an important part of the counselling process, both in terms of the progress of the client and the development of the counsellor, then it is congruent to have self evaluation as a strong theme in the assessment of participants' skills. Similarly, peer-assessment is an excellent way of developing openness, genuineness or congruence as personal qualities; or if the course favours an interpretative model, developing interpretative skills including the ability to give respectful feedback. Some courses

limit peer-assessment and evaluation to giving feedback, both personal feedback and feedback on skills performance. The tutors will always reserve the right to make pass/fail decisions. Other courses, particularly those in the person-centred tradition will place both self and peer assessment in a more central position. They may extend peer assessment to written work as well as skills work and pass/fail decisions may be shared between tutors and course participants with no one individual or group having the right to a veto.

The British Association for Counselling *Code of Ethics and Practice for Trainers* (see pages 9 - 13) states that 'self and peer assessment are encouraged' at 'regular intervals' on counselling courses (Section B4.3)

Activity - Your course assessment.
Try answering the following questions. (It might be more lively if you do this in small groups)

• Are students encouraged to question and become involved in assessment issues?
• What is the theoretical orientation of the course?
•What types of assignment are you expected to complete?
   • Are the assignments congruent with the theoretical approach?
   • Are any elements student-led?
• Is there any peer-assessment?
• Is there any self-assessment?

What should be assessed and how ?

You might think that it is no business of students to go asking such questions. You would be wrong. If counselling courses are serious about self and peer assessment then it is essential that course participants understand the issues behind the assessment of their work. In the cases where courses require trainees to set the criteria by which they will be assessed, it is even more important that trainees understand what elements of knowledge skills and understanding could be assessed and how it might be done.

What should be assessed?

Campbell Purton in 1991 reviewed assessment on four courses (the Facilitator Development Institute diploma [person-centred], the Psychosynthesis and Education Trust diploma, the Westminster Pastoral Foundation diploma [psychodynamic] and the Goldsmiths College MSc). Purton summarised the predominant themes in assessment in terms of the differences between the approaches. This work led me to think that there might be some key issues in the assessment of counselling training that all trainees, regardless of theoretical orientation, might consider when thinking about how *their* course assesses fitness to practise counselling or counselling skills:

- Are trainees capable of working in a way that not only does not abuse the power dynamics of the counselling relationship, but actively seeks to make therapeutic use of these dynamics?
- Are trainees sufficiently self-aware and committed to professional supervision, to ensure that their clients' needs are not superseded by the practitioner's own needs.
- Can trainees balance the needs of professionalism on the one hand with intuitive perception and autonomous action on the other without losing themselves in either to the detriment of the client?
- Can trainees give a good account of their chosen theoretical approach, both written and verbal?
- Can trainees describe the wider theoretical context of their counselling approach?
- Can trainees demonstrate average or good counselling skills or advanced therapeutic skills?
- Have trainees read key texts in counselling theory and practice.
- Is the assessment system fair, consistent and without bias, whilst acknowledging the individual identity of each student and their own learning and assessment needs?

Activity - What do you think should be assessed? It is sometimes better to do this in small groups.

- Having read the above section, what are your priorities for the assessment of counselling skills and counselling?

- Try answering this first as a trainee, second as a client and third as a member of the public concerned about professional standards.

- Is there any difference between these views?

- Who should be listened to when assessments are designed?

- How can fairness and consistency be achieved?

What is competence?

It is one thing to be able to demonstrate counselling skills with clients, it is another to demonstrate that the skills are effectively applied. The term *effective* is the key here and is at the centre of the debate regarding whether skills *as such* should be assessed, or whether the *outcome* of the application of the skills should also be assessed.

The main problem here is that both skills and outcomes are value-laden. That is to say that what might be a skill to a psychodynamic trainer, might not be recognised as a skill to a person-centred trainer, and indeed may be actively discouraged in trainees.

The problem with outcomes is compounded by the difficulty in measuring them, even if we could agree on what outcomes to aim for.

Activity - How would you measure competence? Consider these questions in small groups.

• What are the counselling *skills* that you think it is essential that a counsellor is able to demonstrate?
　• How would you assess these skills?
• What *outcomes* would you look for in order to show the effectiveness of a counsellor's skills?
　• How would you assess these outcomes?
• How would you measure these skills and outcomes fairly and consistently so that trainees can feel safe that they have not been discriminated against?

Tutor assessment

Most of us are familiar with the method of assessment wherein we hand our work in to the tutor then wait for it to be assessed or 'marked' in private with no negotiation or consultation. John Heron (1988) pointed out that assessment is a power issue and since counselling training is partly about understanding power dynamics in relationships, it is important that assessment styles model such concerns appropriately. In other words, some degree of consultation and negotiation would be desirable in counselling assessments. If counsellors are to have empowering relationships with clients, it is appropriate that they are not disempowered during training.

Tutors often have the final say as to whether an individual trainee passes or fails a given piece of work or even the course as a whole. This can be the case even where a fair deal of self and peer assessment are required. The tutors reserve the right to 'pull rank' so to speak on any decisions made by peers. We will look at exceptions to this or alternative ways of making decisions in the *Peer assessment* and *Self assessment* sections below.

Tutors do bring expertise and a different, wider, professional view to the assessment procedure. If the assessment method enables this view to be shared then all participants will benefit. This sharing most often happens when tutors give feedback on individual students' work. A simple grade, plus a 'Good', or 'Could do better' comment (the sort we are used to from school) will not help much, so you will find that your tutors will write several sentences of comments related to your work, probably on a separate piece of paper. This will often be backed up by an opportunity to talk through your work in a one-to-one tutorial.

Tutors can be centrally involved in the assessment of all elements of training and development, including on some courses, the personal development of the trainees. This area of assessment is probably the most sensitive and the most open to accusations of bias through personal discrimination or favour because of the power dynamics of assessment. It is rare that tutors will take such decisions as individuals. The best way to ensure fairness in such cases is to make the assessment a 'staff team' responsibility. Some courses require that this assessment is done in public at community meetings so that any implications for the way power is used by the staff team can be dealt with openly.

Peer assessment
This method of assessment can be applied to all elements of assessment, theory, skills, professional development and personal development. Furthermore it is applied to both written assessment as well as verbal evaluation of counselling skills on a number of courses. There are many types of peer assessment possible and courses will have a position regarding peer assessment and its status (see below) according to a number of factors, including the theoretical orientation of the course.

It is worth reminding readers that BAC 'encourage' peer assessment at regular intervals on counsellor training courses and at least once (if not regularly) on counselling skills courses. The following is a list of some of the possible peer *evaluation* and *assessment* methods that may be found in various combinations on courses. (Here, evaluation is taken to mean appraisal of skills, knowledge, or attributes for the purpose of development only, which does not count towards a pass/fail decision. Assessment is used to mean appraisal which is employed for pass/fail or grading decisions.)

This group represents *evaluation* opportunities:
• Feedback in personal development groups or community meetings regarding personal qualities and attributes.
• Feedback on counselling skills from an observer when practising skills with a fellow student.
• Feedback on a tape recording of counselling skills, practised with a fellow student, from a group of peers.
• Feedback on a tape recording of counselling or counselling skills work with a client.
• Feedback on whether a trainee has met their own, self-determined learning goals (see *Self assessment*, below).
• Feedback on a prepared presentation to the class by all those in the class.

This group represents *assessment* processes:
• Feedback in personal development groups or community meetings regarding personal qualities and attributes *and pass/fail decisions made by consensus in public*.
• Feedback on, *and grading pass/fail of*, a tape recording of counselling or counselling skills practise whether with a fellow student or client.
• Marking of essays and other written work by peers with feedback, *grading and pass/rewrite/ fail decisions being made by the peer assessor*.
• Feedback on whether a trainee has met their own self-determined learning goals and *a pass/*

fail decision made by consensus in public.
• Feedback on and *rating and grading* of a prepared presentation to the class by all those in the class.

The main difference between peer evaluation and peer assessment, regardless of the informal nature of some peer evaluation, is that peer assessment counts for something, it has teeth, and it puts some of the responsibility for maintaining standards on the trainees themselves.

Giving good evaluative feedback is difficult enough for most of us, since we are prone to lapse into polite hollow, meaningless responses. We know that this is useless and soon the whole process becomes stale and worthless. The whole feedback process becomes untrustworthy and then we tend to avoid it.

When peer assessment has teeth, these difficulties would appear to increase, yet it is the experience of many that it gives a sharp edge to the whole process, forcing us to consider our responses more carefully

---

Activity - Peer assessment
Consider the following questions in small groups:

• Could you give and receive challenging yet constructive feedback?
• What difference would it make if pass/fail decisions hung on some of this feedback?
• Would you want to have a hand in telling someone that they had failed the course because they were not good enough in your view, or would you rather the tutors did it?

---

and give them more respectfully. Set against this is the tendency to retreat into an 'I'll pass yours if you pass mine' mentality. The skill of the tutor as facilitator of the educational process is paramount in preventing this from happening and keeping the peer assessment process on track.

Self assessment
If peer assessment seems a novel idea to those of us who are refugees from a traditional education, then self assessment seems very strange indeed. How can an individual assess their own abilities? The whole traditional education system seems to suggest that assessment is an objective process which, in order to be fair and consistent, needs to be put at some distance from the individual in question in order to achieve the kind of neutrality required. Surely, if left to assess ourselves, we would just simply do the minimum required and pass ourselves with flying colours!

That is the fantasy. The reality is, however, that self assessment is a feature of a wide spectrum of counsellor training, not simply the extreme left field of the person-centred approach. There are a few reasons for this:
• Developing and increasing self awareness is at the heart of both the counselling process and the counselling training process. It makes sense, therefore to put self evaluation and even the additional responsibility of self assessment into the mix of assessment methods.
• Any model of counselling based on empowerment might consider it congruent to have some elements of self evaluation and assessment in the course. This also challenges

assumptions about the power dynamics in relationships, whether between client and counsellor or student and tutor.

• Part of the repertoire of skills of a professional counsellor is to be able to monitor and evaluate one's own performance in order both to protect clients and seek continual professional development. One way of developing such skills is by asking trainees to share responsibility through self assessment. This is sometimes referred to as developing an 'internal supervisor'

Staying with the distinction between evaluation and assessment outlined in the previous section, some popular forms of self assessment adopted by courses are as follows: self *evaluation* (when not formally marked or part of a pass/fail decision), and self *assessment* when graded, marked and forming part of the pass/fail criteria:

• Personal journal (may be used to inform individual tutorials but not necessarily handed in and marked).

• Personal learning statements - a written summary of the things learned (and how) during a set period on the course, or a particular activity, or in a set assignment, i.e. 'What I learned from writing this essay was...'

• Self-evaluation - written or verbal evaluation or assessment of, for example, counselling skills demonstrated in a tape recorded interview with a client, possibly using prescribed headings:

'What I liked about this session was...'
'What I didn't like about this sessions was...'
'How I could have improved...'

'Supervision issues raised by this session...' etc.

• Self-assessment statement - a statement presented to the tutors, peers or the course community, explaining why the trainee thinks they are fit to practise, incorporating some of the above ideas, i.e. strengths and weaknesses, things learned, things to work on, personal attributes, etc.

Activity - Self assessment
Try answering the following questions in small groups.

• Do you think that self assessment is congruent with your chosen counselling approach, or the theoretical orientation of your course?

• How do you feel about assessing yourself in general?

• How do you feel about submitting a self assessment statement detailing:

• what you think you have learned,

• your strengths and weaknesses - including   your personal attributes,

• what you think you have to learn next,

• how you think you have used supervision,

• your personal model of counselling and what theories have influenced you to date.

• Would you like to see more or less self assessment on your course?

Some courses place a heavy emphasis on self assessment, and on such courses, a self-assessment statement can run to many thousands of words and form the major course assessment, incorporating an appreciation of the trainee's understanding of theory, their emergent personal counselling style and record of their counselling practise.

Personal growth
There can be no doubt that some trainees have such difficulty containing their own personal material and needs that they would not be able to serve their clients' need in an effective and properly professional manner. However, the prospect of assessing (rather than evaluating) someone's personal growth or development on a counselling course is bound to signal the start of a heated debate. If we take the view that assessment requires a value judgement, then a tutor making a value judgement about someone's personal development would not be congruent with some theoretical approaches. If the course has a requirement that trainees undertake personal therapy during training, the requirement is usually that they attend, *not* that they bring back a satisfactory report from their therapist. (Would it be ethical for therapists to supply one anyway?) If we believe that tutor assessment is a neutral, objective process of arbitration, then some would object to having such a cold, soulless, inhuman process applied to that most human part of their educational development. Some would argue that the person with the least accurate handle on a trainee's personal growth is the tutor, precisely *because* of the power dynamics of the relationship, and the quite reasonable tendency for trainees to present their most adequate selves to tutors, not their most vulnerable selves.

Finally, the issue of having any kind of view at all about another person's personal growth and development lies so close to whether you *like* them or not, and is so open to scrutiny from the power-dynamics-of-the-student-tutor-relationship point of view, that many trainers prefer to tackle this issue indirectly.

The rationale behind indirect methods of assessment is that if a tight enough net of assessment is created, then someone at an inappropriate stage of personal development would not pass through. So we would expect the trainee counsellor's personal development needs to show through into their skills practise with fellow students, their tape recorded work with clients, their supervision, their essay writing or some other aspect of written work. In short, how we are as *people* (and our fitness to be a counsellor) will somehow show up in our other assessments and we would fail on that basis.

- Indirect methods of assessment, then, would include almost all aspects of the assessment schedule, but of particular relevance might be:
  - Feedback on and grading of counselling skills or counselling practice assignments.
  - Supervisors reports.
- Direct methods of assessment of personal development include, starting with the most widely used and accepted:
  - Trainee's personal journal. Many courses have this as an *assessed* piece of work.
  - A report from the trainee's personal therapist.
  - Peer assessment of each trainees' fitness to practise *including* personal qualities and personal development. This will often be done in public at a community meeting or in a small tutorial or seminar group.
  - Tutor assessment of each trainees' fitness to

practise *including* personal qualities and personal development. This is most usually done in private one-to-one tutorials, where one tutor passes on the feedback and assessments made by the whole tutorial team.

• Self assessment of fitness to practise. It is rare, but not unheard of, for a student to fail themselves in this way.

Assessing the personal qualities and personal development of trainees on completion of the course will almost certainly form part of the assessment scheme in some shape or form. Only a tiny minority of courses rely upon formal traditional assessment, such as essays and exams to do this.

Activity - Personal growth assessment. Consider the following questions.

• Is it the expectation on your course that personal growth should not be assessed?
• Do you think that personal growth *should* be assessed?
• Who do you think is best placed to assess a trainee's personal growth?
   • The trainee themselves.
   • Peers.
   • Tutors.
   • Some other person or combination of people.
• What sort of information would be needed before it could be fair?

Making sure it's fair and up to standard

When tutors are busy tutoring and marking in teams scattered around the country it would be easy for them to become isolated and lose their sense of what a 'pass' and 'fail' really means. Two ways of ensuring fairness, consistency and equal standards are firstly making it so that assignments are marked by two tutors, and secondly by appointing an external examiner or moderator to 'oversee' the assessment process.

The External Examiner will be an experienced trainer from another course or institution whose job it is to compare standards between courses, adjudicate in disputes and make sure the marking rules have been fairly applied to all work, see pages 86 & 87.

Ways of assessing the *whole* counsellor

You will only be able to answer the questions in the *Activity box* on page 79 fully if you have been given a complete list of the assignments required on your course together with an explanation of the style or type of each assignment. The BAC Code (pages 9 - 13) requires that trainees are given information before the start of the programme on 'Evaluation and assessment methods used during the programme and the implications of these.' (Section B4.1h.)

The purpose of this schedule of assignments or scheme of assessment is to evaluate all relevant aspects of knowledge, attitudes, skills and understanding that relate to counselling. In other words to make sure that 'whole' or 'well rounded' practitioners are awarded a certificate or diploma. The range of assignments will be chosen to get as many 'angles' or viewpoints on the trainee as

Inside Story 2: *The External Examiner*
Trying to keep standards within and between courses

Janet Tolan

When I am first introduced to course members, I often get the strong impression that they see me as the person who can "fail" them. There is, of course, some reality to this, but the other side of the coin is that I might advise the course team that they are being over harsh in their marking. In fact, an external examiner, assessor, moderator or verifier is employed by the validating or awarding body to make sure that its requirements are met. It is more my job to look at a sample of course members' work than at any one individual, and to say whether the tutors are setting an appropriate standard overall.

There are two main aspects to the business of judging what is or is not an appropriate standard. The most important is matching what the tutors have said on paper with what is happening in practice. In their course documents, the course tutors will have given details about how they are going to satisfy the requirements of the validating body. Each validating body asks for slightly different information. Details such as the number of hours in the course, the course objectives and curriculum, the expertise of the tutors and how the students will be assessed form the core of the course document. In addition, there may be requirements which cover the rooms which are used and other facilities such as library and video equipment.

The course documents are, in effect, a contract between the course tutors and the validating body

and, by extension, between the course tutors and the students. The external examiner is there to make sure that the contract is upheld, particularly with regard to assessment.

Students should be given details of the work they must submit for assessment - essays, case studies, audio or video tapes, book reviews and so on - the number of each and required submission dates. They should also be given details of any penalties for late submission, whether they can re-submit any work which does not meet the required standards and how they can make an appeal or a complaint if they are not satisfied that the course team has "followed the rules".

It is also good practice for the students to be given the marking criteria so that they can see how tutors are making their judgements about a particular piece of work. However, even with the clearest marking criteria, the need for some judgement and interpretation remains. Let us take an example to illustrate the point:

Imagine that one of the criteria against which a video tape is marked is the student's ability to reflect the client's feelings.

Tutor 1: This student is reflecting the client's feelings. I think we should award a pass.

Tutor 2. But I don't think she *is* reflecting feelings. Most of the time, she seems to be just repeating

...continued

Inside Story 2: The External Examiner

Trying to keep standards within and between courses

Janet Tolan

what the client has said.

Tutor 1: But the things she repeats are at least feelings rather than content.

Tutor 2: Well, I think we should be looking for more than that. I'd like our students to be able to pick up on some of the underlying emotions.

When there is disagreement between tutors about how to interpret the marking criteria, they may well call upon the external examiner to help. Sometimes, a discussion will result in a recommendation that the course team makes changes to the criteria to amend or clarify them (for example, *is able to reflect unspoken feelings*).

This brings me to the second aspect of judging whether the standards set by the course are appropriate, i.e. offering my experience of other, similar courses elsewhere. Course tutors are usually keen to make sure that their Certificate or Diploma compares well with others in the field. Conversely, they do not want to withhold certification from someone who would have achieved a 'pass' if they had attended another reputable course.

I have been an external examiner, assessor and moderator for more than ten years and for a range of organisations and courses. Mostly, there is no conflict between the interests of students, tutors, the validating body, future clients of students and the profession as a whole - all benefit from clear, fair assessment procedures and all welcome the involvement of someone external to the organisation to help them achieve this. Even in dealing with an appeal or a complaint, careful investigation will usually show whether or not rules, procedures or agreements have been broken. The tricky part here can be the feelings of the course team if they have been found not to have acted in accordance with the requirements, or students who want something which is outside the contracted offering.

The best scenario, of course, is one in which complaints and appeals do not happen. The course team can help by making all of the requirements and procedures available to students so that they are as open and transparent as possible. Students can help by asking for any information which they do not have, reading everything carefully and querying at an early stage things which in practice do not seem to fit with the paperwork. External examiners can help by reminding tutors of their contract with the validating body and students, and by listening carefully to what students have to say.

In writing this, I wondered why I carry on doing this job when the financial rewards are so poor. Surely, I've done enough of it not to need further notches on my CV? The answer, I think, is twofold: It's part of my own professional development - I always learn something from watching how colleagues work and from listening to other perspectives. And there's nothing quite as satisfying as going into a buzzing learning group and knowing that they're discovering counselling.

possible, covering as many key abilities and attributes as possible.

Over the whole course it is reasonable to expect a mixture of styles of assignment:

- An audio or video tape of your work with peers or clients to demonstrate basic or advanced counselling skills which may be assessed by your peers and your tutor(s) according to criteria laid down by the course tutors, your peers or yourself.
- A self-assessment of your performance on the tape according to some criteria laid down by the tutors, peers or yourself.
- An essay on some aspect of counselling theory.
- An essay on how you have developed your own approach to counselling or using counselling skills.
- An essay on a professional or ethical topic.
- Some kind of self-evaluation statement giving an account of the things you have learned on the course which may have to be passed by your peers.
- Reviews of one or more counselling-related books plus a record of your reading as evidence of the depth and breadth of your reading on the course.
- A presentation on a counselling-related topic made to the rest of your course group and tutors.
- A case study written up and presented to the rest of your course group and tutor(s).
- A dissertation.
- A research proposal or project on some counselling-related area.
- An exam on medical model or psychopathology.

The above is just a selection of the types of assignment most favoured by counselling courses. The exact balance between skills and academic elements in the assessment scheme will depend upon whether the course has a 'practitioner training' emphasis or an 'academic excellence' emphasis. Some trainers take the view that the best preparation for being a professional counsellor is academic rigour and a writing-based assessment, whilst others take the view that a professional counsellor needs to be more proficient in the therapeutic skills of counselling and will base assessment around this. As a very rough general rule, courses in universities tend to be more academic, but there are exceptions. There is a real debate about which is the best way to assess counselling knowledge and skills with good points to be made on both sides, although few trainers advocate a large bias in favour of academic assessment.

The debate has recently been joined by those favouring National Vocational Qualifications. The

Lead Body for Advice, Guidance, Counselling and Psychotherapy are responsible for devising standards for the assessment of competent counselling. (The debate regarding competence vs skills assessment has been very briefly introduced above.) The attempts to look at assessment in terms of competencies and develop standards against which to measure performance has been accelerated by the advent of NVQs and the involvement of the Lead Body. It is difficult at this stage to predict the effect that the NVQ initiative will have on counselling training and assessment, and the whole debate raises strong feelings on both sides.

The search for competencies in counselling does not, however, detract from trainers' attempts to assess the *whole* counsellor or counselling skills practitioner. Whilst the vast majority of trainers will seek to achieve this, exactly how each course sets about the task will vary considerably, influenced mainly by the therapeutic approach adopted by the course.

Activity
Does your training assess the
whole *counsellor?*

• Do you have a copy of the assessment scheme for your course and the criteria used for making pass/fail decisions?
• Is there a balance between academic and skills based assessment?
• Is the scheme congruent with the theoretical approach of the course?
• Do you understand each type of assignment and how to complete them successfully?

Types of assignment in counselling training

I have thought long and hard about how to stop the next section being an annotated list of assignment types, but have resigned myself to the notion that it will be nothing more than that. I would encourage you to read beyond the styles of assignment found on your course. You may find other ways of tackling the same assessment issues inspirational and you *may* be able to negotiate slightly different styles of assessment with your tutors (although do not *expect* that this *will* happen unless your course at least leans towards a person-centred approach.)

The following list is for illustration only (wordages are approximate), course tutors will have their own meanings for some of these assignment titles, or different titles for the same pieces of work. Always check the requirements first. What follows is an indication of what you *might* expect, not best practice, or recommended; simply illustrations.

Written Assignments

1. Book review

Aims: To encourage and provide evidence of reading of counselling-related texts. To encourage critical appraisal of books and articles.

Wordage: Between 500 and 1500 words.

Format: As per book and record reviews in newspapers and magazines. Could be structured in terms of a brief description of the contents, what you think or how you feel about the book, how useful it is for trainees on your course, would you recommend it?

For extra help: look at book reviews in *Counselling* the Journal of the British Association for Counselling, or *Counselling News.*

Inside Story 3: *The Tutor*
Assessment on a Diploma Course: The case for exams

Alan Frankland

I'm Alan Frankland, Principal Lecturer in Counselling and Psychotherapy at the Nottingham Trent University. When we designed our Postgraduate Diploma we created a "Portfolio Assessment System" which attempts, as all assessments should, to provide a fair measure of individual achievements within identifiable standards whilst having a generally benign effect on the course by remaining congruent with counselling values. Thus our assessment system seeks to respect the competence and autonomy of the learner, acknowledge diversity, complexity and process and not assume that there are "right answers" in human affairs. It has to do this whilst meeting the needs and demands of University procedures and expectations which, on the whole, still operates as if there are things to know, right answers, and externally evaluated paradigms of organised knowledge, conveniently paralleling the hierarchical structures of the institution itself.

We think a congruent assessment procedure can only be achieved in counsellor training when course members are given choice and **responsibility** through **negotiation,** not only of assessment subjects/topics, but also of the form assignments take. So long as an assignment has clear (and agreed) goals and assessment criteria, it can be fairly assessed whether it is in a traditional or more innovative form- and wherever practicable (against constraints of time and issues like confidentially) course members share the responsibility for their own assessments and that of their peers.

If that seems faintly radical you may be surprised to learn that the system also includes an unseen exam during the closing stages of the course. Some educational liberals protest that exams are "just a test of memory", "meaningless" and reactionary - wholly unsuited to the education and assessment of adults, but all that misses the point here. It is perfectly possible to set an examination that tests only candidates' working knowledge; and sensible to recognise that any trade or profession requires a fair amount of such knowledge.

Counselling certainly does: counsellors make moment to moment ethical, organizational and situational decisions every working day. Whilst coursework assignments may be sound ways to evolve the understanding that underpins these decisions, the acid test of whether practice knowledge is soundly embedded is when we are asked to respond rapidly, as we are when faced with new clients and unexpected situations - or in an exam.

An exam is also an antidote to over-specialisation. Even in a negotiated system, some course members may wish to concentrate all their energies on one or two topics. Sometimes the commitment this brings is an excellent stimulus

...continued

Inside Story 3: The tutor

Assessment on a Diploma Course -
The case for exams

Alan Frankland

for learning across the board but specialised assignments won't ensure that the breadth of learning is adequately assessed. An examination towards the end, drawing topics of a fundamental nature from across the range will address this - either by encouraging course members to keep some breadth to their studies or by demonstrating to assessors that someone who had seemed to overspecialise had nevertheless addressed a range of fundamental issues through those studies.

There is also the point that an assessment package containing a wider range of procedures will probably be more accurate for a wider range of candidates. Ironically, this was the argument used twenty years ago to broaden exam-only assessment systems by bringing in "coursework", but in some areas the liberal pendulum swung so far that the range again became narrowed, by the exclusion of unseen methods.

We decided it was time to allow the pendulum to swing back (just a bit), and so far our experience of using an exam within a largely negotiated system has been successful: some course members even enjoyed it!

2. Skills directory
Aims: To demonstrate knowledge of individual counselling skills. To help focus understanding of the origin and applicability of individual counselling skills.
Wordage: Between 1000 and 3000 words
Format: A list of counselling skills with each skill expanded under, for example, the following headings; title, description of skill, originated or first described by...(reference), most associated with...(name of counselling approach), circumstances under which skill is used, possible effects of skill.

3. Examinations
Aims: To test knowledge of a range of counselling issues.
Wordage/Time: Between one and three hours.
Format: Can be 'seen' where candidates can see the questions beforehand and prepare for them, or 'unseen', where candidates get no prior sight of the paper.
For extra help: See pages 90 & 91, and 69 - 71.

4. Essay
Aims: To test understanding of more complex issues, e.g. describing theory, comparing theoretical approaches, discussing ethical dilemmas, explaining how theory relates to practise.
Wordage: Between 1500 and 5000 words. Certificate or counselling skills courses will have a lower wordage requirement than diploma courses. Courses sometimes make distinctions between 'short essays' and 'long essays', although each course will have different requirements for this.
Format: Traditional essay format, e.g. title; free-

Model Answer 2: *Book Review (500 words)*

BEING AND BELONGING - Group, Intergroup and Gestalt by Gaie Houston, 1993, John Wiley & Sons, Chichester.

I found this book very readable and thoroughly enjoyed it. Not only because it is a fascinating observation of groups, and an informative illustration of gestalt in theory and in practice but because it constitutes absorbing reading. The author is a gestalt therapist and teacher, an experienced group facilitator and has written many plays which have been broadcast by the BBC. She puts all these skills together in this book and has produced a polished and highly original text.

The book is an enthralling portrayal of a fictional group of nine, whose leader is absent, and who are together for five days. The characters in the group come from different theoretical orientations and different cultures. There is Orminda, Irish, who was trained by Carl Rogers; Grace, British West Indian, Gestalt trained; Pierre, French, Psychoanalysis (influenced by Bion) trained; Birdie, Swedish, Gestalt trained; Manfred, German, Family Therapy training; Sohan, Indian (Asian), Art Therapist; Chuck, an Australian Psychiatrist; Annie English, Kleinian Psychotherapist, and Sappho, Greek, Psychodrama training. Quite a combination!

We learn in this book about different approaches to group behaviours and we are also encouraged to consider what it is about people's personalities that draw them to specific theories of human behaviour. The group's development at the beginning is tense and argumentative and is recorded by the group members and also by the absent leader. The creativity and destructiveness is graphically shown and the characters come alive and you begin to really care about Orminda's grief, Sappho's selfishness, Pierre's aloofness, Annie being the fat older woman, Grace's isolation in her strength and Manfred's refusal to truly commit himself to the group.

As in all groups, issues of belonging are central to this book. Group members try to retain their individuality whilst at the same time wanting desperately to be part of the group. This process is excellently portrayed by Houston and shows all the mistrust and anxiety that is experienced by the individual group members and then as trust develops it is wonderful to hear the true communication coming through as the group members listen and respond to one another. The theme of belonging is explored not only in the group of nine but with other groups who are meeting at the same time.

Whilst Houston's own orientation is firmly gestalt she does examine other theories. Thus we have observations from Foulksian, Kleinian and Jungian viewpoints, as well as Bion and systems theories. My only criticism of this book is that Rogers is mentioned only twice and yet to me Orminda, who was trained by Rogers, came through as the heroine. Is this my bias? I don't think so.

My overall impression of this book is that it gave an excellent understanding of group process which related to the beginnings, middles and endings of all groups. Although Houston's starting point is "belonging seems so often in a capitalist culture, to imply exclusivity, property, curtailment of freedom" we are left at the end with the sense that true communication is possible between people of different cultures and different beliefs. All be it an academic book I would recommend this book as an excellent bedtime read.

flowing writing; references and bibliography, diagrams or illustrations permitted but sub-headings usually discouraged.

For extra help: See pages 105 - 123.

5. *Dissertation*

Aims: To demonstrate ability to assemble and link carefully considered descriptions or evaluative arguments on selected theoretical or practise-related issues, or to pursue dilemmas and contradictions to meaningful conclusions. To search appropriate literature and give evidence of wide reading. To achieve these aims through extended writing.

Wordage: Between 5000 and 15,000 words.

Format: Traditional dissertation format, maybe more relaxed structure permitted, flowing writing, diagrams and illustrations permitted, sub-headings or chapter headings encouraged, e.g. title; introduction; literature search; chapters; conclusions; references; bibliography.

For extra help: See pages 105 - 123 & 134.

6. *Case study*

Aims: To develop or give evidence of appreciation of professional issues, client practise issues and relationship of both to theory. To demonstrate ability to write in suitable style for fellow professionals. To demonstrate ability to communicate therapeutic decisions to others.

Wordage: Between 1000 and 3000 words.

Format: Can take many forms dependent upon purpose and theoretical approach, although a selection from the following would probably be appropriate. Description of context and demographic details of client e.g., age; presenting problem; referral path; number of sessions; setting, age, sex, etc. Initial diagnosis if

appropriate to therapeutic approach. Description and evaluation of sessions in terms of efficacy and progress or changes in client. Explanation and justification of methods and approaches used. Supervision issues raised by client work. Conclusions or suggestions for continuation of therapy, including referral possibilities if appropriate.

For extra help: see pages 123 - 132.

7. *Self-appraisal - personal journals*

Aims: To encourage and assess personal reflection and awareness of a range of aspects of the self-development process. To demonstrate commitment to ongoing counsellor development.

Wordage: Variable.

Format: Variable, some courses provide loose structure or suggest headings or areas for special attention. Most leave unstructured for creative interpretation by writer. Illustrations, drawings, poems, prose, notes, etc., all permitted if not encouraged.

For extra help: See page 133.

8. *Self-appraisal - personal learning statements*

Aims: To demonstrate awareness of setting personal learning goals, monitoring performance, and noting when personal learning goals have been met.

Wordage: Variable. Some personal learning statements are of dissertation length and form the major summative assessment for a course. Some are very short (around 100 - 500 words) and are handed in with each piece of work to log the learning goals achieved with that particular piece of work).

Format: Again, variable. Courses usually give guidelines for completion of personal learning statements, with acceptable sub-heads etc. It is

Model Answer 3: *Transcript and evaluation (extract)*

The following is an extract from a transcript and evaluation of a tape recorded counselling session with a client. Although the transcript is very loosely based on a couple of real clients, with all the characters (including the counsellor) changed and, on occasions, the action too; it is completely unrecognisable. There are no tutor comments in this panel so that you can practice your peer-evaluation skills. What do you think of the student's powers of self-evaluation, given the transcript. This is only an extract, but should give a good enough idea to enable you to assess both the performance in the session and the evaluation of it. It doesn't matter whether you read the transcript or the evaluation first.

Evaluation

Introduction

This is the 6th session with Jim. He is unemployed and married with three children, girls aged 4, 16 and 19. Jim was referred to me by the GP because he was having difficulty coming to terms with his 16 year old daughter's mental illness (diagnosed as schizophrenia) and the impact on the rest of the family. I see Jim weekly at the surgery, and because he spends his days at home, he looks after the 4 year old whilst his wife does a part-time job. The first session was difficult because he brought his 4 year-old daughter with him. After I explained the nature of counselling, he arranged childcare for the morning he comes to the surgery.

The session

In this, as in previous sessions, Jim explores his relationship with his daughter. He feels that she only shows the 'mad' bits of herself to him, as if she doesn't want him to know that there's anything OK about her.

Early on in the session I was able to reflect Jim's sadness but totally missed the anger that he felt. Although I was able to be respectful with the response 'All your dreams for Alice, all your plans for her have been put on hold.' I feel that Jim could have used the session to explore his anger if I had captured it better then. Another feature of this session was that it felt very 'heavy' with lots of heavy silence. I got very close at one point - a little too close maybe. Immediately, Jim changed tack and talked about his older daughter who is a great success in life. He quickly moved on to talk about helping out at the day centre summer fete. I responded with 'Does it feel easier to talk about this than to talk about your painful feelings?'

I realised that the question forced him to look at his behaviour and he looked very uncomfortable. I could have kicked myself - I could have phrased it much better, maybe saying 'So its not been bad really and somehow it feels almost easier to talk about this than feelings', which would have been a more accurate reflection of what he was doing (I think). The interesting thing is that he seemed to move on to the edge of his feelings at this point, but I still think I could have been less clumsy.

I like Jim a lot and find myself caring deeply for him in the session. I think I might be 'too soft' on him, too gentle. The excerpt above might be an example of this. He doesn't remind me of anyone I can think of, but I just feel his desperation and disappointment so vividly it's almost unbearable. This is an issue I must take to supervision.

Model Answer 3: *Transcript and evaluation (extract)*
(continued)

Transcript

Five minutes into session.

Jim (Client): Its just as though she keeps her best, er.. most normal bits for other people. If she shows that to other people, why not me?

Pat (Counsellor): You look sad as you say that.

Silence

J: It does hurt.

Silence

J: and I suppose I feel quite angry about it.

Silence

J: I'm angry at life.

P: All your dreams for Alice, all your plans for her have been put on hold.

Silence

J: I don't know, maybe she'll get there in the end.

P: The way you said that, it was like, 'Maybe she will get there one day, but I don't really believe it.'

J: No, no I used to believe it...when she...gets over this....

Silence

J: I must admit I've got to the stage where I don't think she ever will...

P: It's really difficult for you having to come to terms with 'This may be it.'

J: Mmm.

P: This is my daughter, I love her, I want her to be well.

J: You hear about other people's children, like my brother's little girl said she wants to be a nurse when she grows up. Betty, her mum's a nurse, they get it all from their parents, so why does Alice...?

P: Alice has got this from me, I can blame myself, I can take all the responsibility. Is that what you're saying?

Long silence.

J: No I don't mind what they are as long as they're happy.

Silence

J: Jane had her first show at college - you know she's doing fashion design or something...you know, clothes. Anyway she was full of it last week. She's at college in London - we had trouble at first with her down there but...anyway that's another story. Where was I yes, ah...yes she wanted us to go down but we couldn't go because of the garden party...no, 'fete' it's called. I did this 'Throw a wet sponge' stall. We had a great day, everyone there, and with Jane's good show - I'm not sure what it was, but we're going to it when they do it after her exams in July...they do it all again. It's great.

P: Does it feel easier to talk about that than talk about your feelings?

Silence

J: *(Laughs)* Yeah I suppose it does really.

P: It feels like the alternative is so painful that, you know 'I want to keep it on one side, away from other happy things.'

Silence

J: I can't...I can't give in to it.

P: It feels like I'll crumble.

J: Oh dear...I don't want to...*(Eyes fill up)* excuse me.. I suppose I try not to think about it.

P: I don't want to cry in front of Pat today.

J: Yes I feel so weak about this thing....helpless.

Silence

sometimes necessary to state which aims or goals have been achieved by reference to course documents. These may have to be negotiated with a course tutor.

9. *Self-appraisal - skills self-evaluation*

Aims: To develop and demonstrate self-awareness and ability to evaluate own counselling skills, strengths and weaknesses in counselling practise.

Wordage: Between 1000 and 5000.

Format: Skills evaluations usually relate to a tape-recorded counselling session, either with a client or fellow course participant. Some courses require fixed headings to be followed, others an unstructured piece of free flowing writing.

For extra help: See page 94 & 95.

10. *Transcripts*

Aims: To facilitate and enhance self-evaluation and assessment of counselling skills.

Wordage: Variable.

Format: A transcript is a written record of the spoken content of a counselling or counselling skills session. It is usually typed and annotated with any comments that will help explain difficult to understand passages. Transcripts are notorious for taking literally hours to complete. Transcribing 30 minutes of dialogue will take around 3 hours concentrated work, plus the time taken for typing it up.

For extra help: Strong coffee and headache pills!

11. *Reading log*

Aims: To encourage a methodical approach to reading. To keep a record of counselling-related books read during the course. To provide a useful record for references.

Wordage: Variable depending upon format.

Format: A chronological or alphabetical list or directory (new page for each letter of alphabet) of counselling-related books read. Annotate as desired (e.g. contents, brief review of useful chapters or quotes), but as a minimum keep full reference details, plus the dates the book was started and finished.

For extra help: none needed, this is a very simple assignment, designed to be useful and tailored to student needs and preferences.

12. *Placement report*

Aims: To summarise and review learning on placement. Possible aims include, learning to work in a team, learning to work in an organisation with values different from those of counselling (e.g. a college or hospital). Learning the management, logistics and procedures of counselling, e.g. appointments, referrals, client absences, etc.

Wordage: Variable depending upon structure of report, 2000 - 5000 words.

Format: Can incorporate other assignments such as client log and client records or extracts from client records. Structure depends upon course requirements and student preferences, but could include, description of placement organisation, nature of referrals, number of clients seen plus details of client statistics, e.g. presenting problems, number of sessions per client, outcomes etc. May have a personal learning statement appended.

12. *Client log/records*

Aims: To keep a record of clients seen, including client absences. To prepare for keeping professional records for future accreditation. Evidence of supervised client practice.

Wordage: Variable.

Format: Simple record of client identifier and any

demographic details necessary,, time; date; duration of interview(s), record of did not attends (DNAs); reasons why and action taken.

For extra help: example on page 55.

14. Client notes

Aims: To meet possible placement requirements (some organisations require notes to be kept in a certain format and these will be randomly audited. To demonstrate ability to keep useful and accurate notes of sessions. To demonstrate trainee has engaged with ethical issues regarding confidentiality as they apply to client notes. Evidence of trainee using client notes and personal records to facilitate case presentations and supervision.

Wordage: variable.

Format: This type of assignment will vary depending upon the therapeutic approach of the course, some may require medical style notes, medical model classifications or other systems of labelling clients. Others would require notes focusing on feelings of the counsellor about their own work.

For extra help: examples on page 55.

Skills assessments - tape recordings

A popular and convenient way of assessing counselling skills is to use audio or video tape recordings. Once recorded, the sessions can be transcribed and subjected to trainee self-assessment, peer assessment or tutor assessment or all three. Skills assessments are often done in small groups with a tutor present so that feedback can be given by peers and tutors.

1. Tape recording of trainee-trainee sessions

Aims: To assess counselling skills or advanced therapeutic skills in as realistic a setting as possible , in this case where one student is acting as client and the other student is acting as counsellor or counselling skills practitioner.

Time: 30 - 60 minutes for session, 30 - 90 minutes for assessment if done in peer group.

Format: Trainees are usually required to make one tape at certificate or counselling skills level and more than one tape at diploma level. Trainees may be asked to select a suitable tape from those that have been made, complete a self-evaluation and present it to peers, tutors or both for feedback and assessment. The tape may be assessed according to pre-determined course criteria or student self-determined criteria. Assurances and precautions will be required for storage and treatment of confidential material.

For extra help: These tape sessions require special management - see 'Learning from and with peers', page 37.

2. Tape recordings of trainee-client sessions

Aims: As above, except that real clients are used. To give insight into and practice in 'real' counselling settings (rather than in course atmosphere) and all associated professional issues, trainee anxiety, etc.

Time: 30 - 60 minutes for session, 30 - 90 minutes for assessment if done in peer group.

Format: See comments above. Particular note must be made of efforts to do the presentation in an ethically acceptable way viz client permission and anonymity. Further precautions may have to be made for storage and treatment of confidential material.

For extra help: See 'Learning from clients and supervisors', page 40.

Presentations

Popular on diploma courses, presentations by students, either singly or in twos and threes can be a daunting prospect, but usually end up being a terrific learning experience.

1. Case study

Aims: To develop case writing and presenting skills. To demonstrate ability to identify and verbally communicate salient points of client casework to peers/professionals. To develop and demonstrate ability to structure work within time limits and draw ideas to meaningful conclusions.

Wordage/time: Variable words, around 30 - 60 minutes presentation/discussion time.

Format: Presentation to small or medium-sized group of peers and tutors. Trainee selects a case for presentation and discussion. Presentation may be supported by written material. Trainee will probably be expected to manage and develop the ensuing discussion. Ethical considerations may form part of the assessment, i.e., how trainee deals with confidentiality/anonymity as it relates to the presentation. Group are often required to complete evaluation/feedback sheets as part of the assessment.

For extra help: See page 146.

2. Workshop/input session

Aims: To develop presentation skills. To demonstrate ability to organise ideas on a counselling-related topic and communicate them to an audience. To develop and demonstrate ability to structure work within time limits and draw ideas to meaningful conclusions.

Time/wordage: Appropriate number of words will vary. 60 - 180 minutes presentation time/ workshop duration.

Format: Trainees are expected to select a counselling-related topic (and usually get it approved by tutor) as the subject of a presentation lasting anywhere between 1 and 3 hours. Sometimes the presentations are organised and given by pairs or small teams. Content and methods can vary according to course requirements and trainee choice. Workshops will usually be more interactive than straightforward presentations. Exercises and discussion will be part of the task and trainees may support the activity with handouts and other printed material such as exercises and references or bibliography.

For extra help: See pages 142 & 148.

3. Viva or oral examination

Aims: To test knowledge and understanding in a 'live' setting without supporting notes and materials.

Wordage/time: Between 15 - 30 minutes.

Format: One to one (rarely, two assessors or examiners). Although this form of assessment is rare, some courses use it to resolve marking disputes or borderline cases (if a student is close to failing) or if a student has through illness or incapacity been unable to complete other elements of the assessment schedule.

For extra help: See page 147.

Supervision

I have included supervision as an assignment in its own right because attendance at supervision and making appropriate use of it are *requirements* not recommendations for training as a professional counsellor at diploma level.

1. Supervision

Aims: To develop awareness of the benefits of supervision and the ability to use supervision effectively. To monitor professional and ethical practice. To secure commitment to ongoing professional development.

Time: Varies from course to course, but to stay within BAC recommendations, should be at least 1 hour supervision to every 5 hours client work.

Format: Individual supervision is one-to-one with an appointed supervisor, group supervision is in small groups with the time being divided for calculation purposes on a pro-rata basis. Supervision is a regular commitment and must be continued post qualification. If you wish to become a BAC individually accredited counsellor, you must receive a minimum of 1.5 hours supervision per month for a minimum of three years after you have successfully completed your diploma course.

For extra help: see BAC *Code of Ethics and Practice for the Supervision of Counsellors*. Also *The Art, Craft and Tasks of Counselling Supervision, Part 1: Making the most of Supervision*, by Brigid Proctor and Francesca Inskipp.

2. Supervisors' reports

Aims: To assess commitment to and appropriate use of supervision. To monitor and provide evidence of continuing professional and ethical practice.

Wordage: Variable between 1000 and 2000 words, written by supervisor.

Format: Can follow headings provided by course team or be in a format determined by supervisor. Usually short. The supervisor may make the report available to the trainee, but some courses and/or supervisors require a confidential report.

For extra help: Talk to your supervisor or tutors about the requirements.

3. Supervisee reports

Aims: To monitor learning through supervision. To assess commitment to and appropriate use of supervision. To monitor and provide evidence of continuing professional and ethical practice.

Wordage: Variable between 1000 - 5000 words.

Format: This is essentially a self-assessment task. Can be a short piece of work following course-determined headings, or a longer dissertation-like piece. It may include a client log or case notes if appropriate, and a log of supervision - times, dates, content. The focus will most likely be on how the trainee used supervision, including an account of some or all of the sessions. A self-learning statement (what I learned from supervision) may also be appropriate, or extracts from a personal journal.

For extra help: See *The Art, Craft and Tasks of Counselling Supervision, Part 1: Making the most of Supervision*, by Proctor and Inskipp.

Research/Projects

1. Research proposal

Aims: To raise awareness of research issues in counselling. To encourage 'research-mindedness'. To assess ability to plan research and write a proposal for prospective study.

Wordage: Varies between 1000 and 3000 words. Exceptionally, can be longer if it includes a literature review or extended appreciation of methods.

Format: As the title implies, this is a proposal to do something, i.e. a piece of research. Research

Inside Story 4: *The Supervisor*
Supervising The Trainee Counsellors' Practice

Rose Cameron

I was really shocked the first time I noticed a diploma student trembling at the beginning of our initial supervision session. I am regretful that the profession has favoured the word 'supervision' with its authoritarian connotations, rather than 'professional consultancy'. I want my supervisees to see me as a supportive resource, not as a source of judgement.

It gives me real pleasure to watch supervisees move from being apprehensive to honest, vulnerable and challenging. How quickly students use supervision well depends very much upon what they understand its purpose to be, and I notice differences in the attitudes students come with, depending on the course they are on. My task of facilitating useful supervision is much easier if the student has had some initial training in what supervision is, and how to get the most out of it. It is somewhat harder if I am formally required to assess their work and pass or fail them. If I do write a report on a supervisee I ask them to assess themselves first, and never send the report off without the student seeing it. It is important to me that supervisees feel they can bring their disasters and despondencies to supervision without fear of judgement, and that they know that one of the functions of supervision is to nurture and restore the counsellor.

Whether the student has chosen, or been allocated, me as a supervisor, who pays for the supervision and whether I am required to send their college reports on their practice, are all factors that potentially affect our relationship. I suggest that we regularly make time to review our relationship and the process of supervision. I see reviews as an opportunity for the supervisee to assess me, and to consider whether I am providing the kind of supervision they want and find useful. I have found that just asking this question is valuable in itself, and encourages supervisees to be active in asking for what they want.

As a supervisor I sometimes want something from supervisees. My most frequent desire is simply for contact. I have found that students sometimes delay making their first appointment for months. Unless I contact them, I have no idea if they are seeing clients without supervision, or having difficulties setting up a work practice. When I check out why they are not coming for supervision, I usually find that they are not considering the possibility that I may be able to help with this, or want to save their supervision sessions for when they are seeing clients. I am in fact very happy to spend a few minutes on the phone suggesting possible placements.

...continued
Inside Story 4: *The Supervisor*
Supervising The Trainee Counsellors' Practice

Rose Cameron

Sometimes I find myself in the position of asking supervisees to take a break from seeing clients altogether, or, more commonly to stop working with a particular client. I often feel varying degrees of anxiety over how this will be received by the supervisee. Sometimes it is met with relief, and has often provided the supervisee with a really important piece of learning.

As my experience as a supervisor grows, I am becoming aware of some patterns in the supervision that I do with all supervisees, not just trainee counsellors. For instance, I am sure there is some relationship between my development as a supervisor and the development of my supervisees as counsellors. It is issues like this, and other issues that come up in my practise as a counsellor, that I take to my own supervisor.

Proposals are echoes from the days when getting funding for research was much more likely than today. It's a bit like a business plan that you might take to a bank manager when asking for a loan. It says what you plan to do, why it's such a good thing and what contribution the results might make to the greater body of counselling knowledge. In short - is this research a good idea? Headings such as; Title (this *is* important), Introduction and rationale, method(s), materials, participants, ethical considerations, possible analysis of results, References and Bibliography, Appendices.

For extra help: See *An Incomplete Guide to Qualitative Research Methods for Counsellors*, by Sanders and Liptrot or *Doing Your Research Project* by Judith Bell

2. Research report

Aims: To develop research skills and assess the ability to conduct and report valid research.

Wordage: Between 3000 - 7000 words.

Format : Differs from a proposal in that it is reporting what *was* done. Usually follows headings such as Abstract, Introduction, Literature Review, Method, (including materials, participants, sampling methods etc.) Ethical Considerations, Results and Analysis, Discussion, References and Bibliography, Appendices.

For extra help, this is a specialised assignment which will benefit from more focused reading. In addition to Sanders and Liptrot and Bell (above), try *An Incomplete Guide to Basic Research Methods and Data Collection for Counsellors*, by Sanders and Liptrot.

Presentation of your work

Some course regulations require that assignments

follow certain guidelines as far as presentation is concerned. These presentation requirements can range from needing two copies of everything through to having everything typed with certain spacing and some long pieces of work, i.e. dissertations, bound in a certain style.

Presentation requirements should be reasonable in the sense that they do not push assignments beyond the limits of access or affordability. Having to get your dissertation typed and bound in a certain style can be a costly business (around £30 - £50) Whilst an increasing number of people have home computers, word processors or typewriters, many do not, so make sure you find someone who can type your work for you (be sure to proof read it) or add an extra amount to cover typing to your estimate of the total cost of the course.

Do take the presentation of your work seriously for two good reasons:

1. How you present your work may say something about how you feel about it; how good you think it is, how much value *you* put on it. Don't undervalue your work with scrappy presentation. If you think your work is good, then present it well.

2. Most of the presentation requirements asked for by tutors have practical reasons, e.g. typed work is *much* easier to read than lots of different handwriting styles. After you've read the fifteenth three thousand word essay, you'd insist that they were typed too!

For more on techniques of presentation see pages 114, 141 and 142.

Did you know...

what psychologists have found out about arousal and performance? **5**

How good we are at anything depends to some extent upon how aroused we are. Psychologists think of arousal as being on a scale from deep sleep (low arousal) to high excitement or panic (high arousal). We can be not aroused enough for a particular task - too tired or sleepy to drive safely, too excited to reading instructions carefully, too anxious to concentrate on listening properly. Each task requires a particular level of arousal and is subject to a relationship best described in the graph opposite. It is called the *Yerkes-Dodson Law.* Complex tasks, such as studying (or counselling!) require a lower level of arousal than simple tasks, and the arousal curve is shorter, allowing less margin of error.

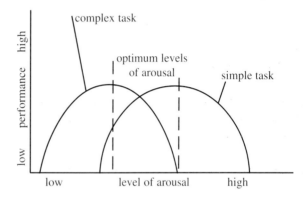

To this must be added our individual characteristics, i.e. whether we prefer or need certain levels of arousal in order to complete certain tasks. This is where we see athletes shouting and stamping to 'psych themselves up' before a big event in to get to the top of the arousal curve. At other times people may need to relax in order to reach the optimum level of arousal.

How can we use these findings?

We might experience something similar when we study - some people need to be moderately aroused in order to concentrate on study, so will put music on or drink coffee (caffeine is a stimulant). Other people will require lower levels of arousal in order to concentrate and so will want absolute quiet with no disturbances. Any kind of performance related to study will be affected by our level of arousal, sitting an exam, giving a presentation, remembering information, or concentrating on reading. It is not simply a matter of 'calming down', in order to do better. Sometimes we might need to 'psyched-up' like the athlete. You will need to sense your own needs, get feedback from others and learn from your own experience in order to get it right for yourself. This is yet another example where the first step is greater self-awareness so that you can change your habits to improve your performance.

Hints and Tips 5

1. Be active in understanding the purpose and form of assessment on your course.

2. Is your course assessing skills, knowledge and understanding? Does the course assess competencies (where the *outcome* of the skill is assessed as well as the skill itself?

3. There are likely to be three types of assessment on your course, each represented to varying degrees depending upon the theoretical orientation of the training:
   tutor assessment, peer assessment and self assessment.
   Are you familiar with each one?

4. Does your course lean towards one or another of these methods or is there a balance?

5. Does your course have an external examiner and/or course consultant?

6. Get hold of a copy of the complete schedule of assignments for your course, complete with handing-in dates.

7. Does your course try to assess the *whole counsellor*?
   • Is there a range of written and non-written assignments tapping in to the various elements of skill, knowledge and understanding in counselling and counselling skills?

8. Become familiar with all of the requirements of all of the assignments in good time to meet deadlines.

9. Try to extend your awareness to the area of arousal. What conditions suit you best for studying - do you work best with a high or low arousal level? What can you do to make your surroundings fit your arousal requirements?

Skills and Techniques for Written Assignments

6

Writing is a form of communication between the writer and the reader. So you, the writer, must aim to communicate your thoughts and ideas to the reader as clearly and efficiently as possible, in a way that not only answers the question asked but that also benefits you too, in that you actually learn something from it, either to be used as part of your professional or personal development, or to be reproduced at a later date in an exam (if your course has examinations as part of the assessment). Remember that assessments are not done for their own sake, they are designed to be of use to you in your learning. They are additional learning opportunities, so use them to learn new material, refine or revise your understanding of old material, integrate new and old material, or review old material to get a new perspective on it.

Essays

A large portion of the assessed work on any course is in the form of essays. Even if the assessment is not strictly an essay (maybe it's a long structured question) the same rules apply. Any assignment has the habit of creeping up on you so that you're left with only an hour or so on the night before the deadline. If you work best under pressure then no doubt you'll be familiar with this way or working and will have your own way of 'producing the goods'. But in an ideal situation, in order to do justice to yourself you really need to start well in advance of the deadline. Mulling ideas over in your head can start as soon as you get the titles. Most students look upon essays as a long-winded and sometimes inappropriate form of assessment. Whilst this may be true, they can also be used to your advantage. It is important that you *interact* with the material that you are studying. Essays provide an ideal opportunity for you to interact with the material, re-organise it, re-jig your notes, incorporate novel material etc. Essays can be used to help on your programme of learning and revision.

As already mentioned essays can be looked on as a form of *communication* between you and your tutor, and for most of us they are a form of communication that needs to be refined, for example, if someone asks you a question, you need to first of all listen to what they are saying and understand the question, secondly you need to consider the points that are relevant to your answer and organise them into a coherent reply and finally you need actually to speak the words in a clear, concise communication. The same three stages roughly apply to writing essays and in this case are:

1. Read and understand the question.
2. Collect and organise your material.
3. Give your answer by writing the essay.

1. Read and understand the question.
To say 'Read the question' sounds rather obvious;

of course everybody reads the question ! Whilst this may be so there is often a gap between simply *reading* the question and *understanding* it. So how can you increase your chances of understanding exactly what is being asked?

You are sometimes asked to make a choice:
'Write an essay on ONE of the following topics'
is a common instruction. You have here the chance to demonstrate your knowledge about a subject together with perhaps your own views on the material you are handling. It is obvious that whenever possible, you should choose a topic about which you are informed, enthusiastic, and can find, if you require it, suitable supportive material; it's no good choosing an essay where all the books you need to help you are out of the library. But you could of course choose a subject you know nothing about in order to further your learning.

It is sometimes worthwhile discovering what is required of answers to several of the essay topics set before firmly committing yourself to one. Doing this may prevent you from working on a topic, only to reach a dead-end. Again a discussion between the tutor and yourself about the implications of the essay topics can be extremely useful in preventing you from proceeding on the wrong track.

You can help yourself by examining carefully the essay title, perhaps highlighting what you think are the important words in the title, A common criticism of students' essays is that they include too much irrelevant material, so try having an essay question always in front of you, that is, the topic worded precisely as it was given to you and not an approximation. A big piece of paper with the essay title written in large letters with the significant words underlined in colour, or ringed, can help you to avoid digressions. It can help if you ask yourself at regular intervals, "Am I answering the question as set?"

There are always two components in any essay title (the same goes for exam questions).
• One part tells you the subject area involved.
• The other tells you what to do with it.
For example you may be asked to describe, discuss, summarise or illustrate with examples any given topic. Your first task is to understand what the question is asking and then *do only that which is asked*. On the next page are some of the most frequently used terms in essays and questions. Read the essay title looking for these key terms and the ones which will help you identify the subject matter.

2. Collect and organise your material

Just as an essay that is produced by a student is the result of a personal response to a stimulus (that is, the question set), so it is that each student has her own individual way of planning her work. The key word here is *plan. Whilst* there is no strong evidence to indicate that one method of planning necessarily creates a better final product, it is true to say that *planning* will result in a better product. It is also clear that most of us, when we can get our acts together enough to make a plan, go through some or all of the steps referred to below. In the planning stage, some prefer to write down a great many notes, whereas others process the material in their minds, or on the back of an envelope. Each of us decides on the methods we think best suit us.

Words commonly used in essay titles

Compare: Look for similarities between.

Contrast: Look for differences between. When used with *compare* you will be expected to reach a conclusion about which idea or approach is preferable.

Criticise: Give your judgement about the merit of theories or opinions, or about the truth of facts. Back your judgement by a discussion of the evidence or reasoning involved. It is never enough simply to state your own opinion.

Define: Give the meaning of.

Describe: Give a detailed or graphic account of.

Discuss: Investigate or examine by argument, give reasons for and against and examine the implications.

Distinguish: Explain the difference.

Evaluate: Judge the importance of.

Explain: Make plain, account for and give reasons for.

Illustrate: Explain the meaning (or possible meaning) of; make clear and explain. (This does not mean simply 'use diagrams or pictures'!!)

Interpret: Explain the meaning in your own words.

Justify: Give reasons to support an argument or action.

Outline: Give the main features or general principles of a topic, *omitting minor details.*

Relate: Retell a story or it can also mean show the relationship between one thing and another.

State: Present in a brief, clear form.

Summarise: Give a concise account of the chief points of a matter, *omitting the details and examples.*

Trace: Show how something has developed from beginning to end.

You could, for example, jot down relevant ideas as they come to you, and if you're really organised, keep them in a folder. Or perhaps relevant points might arise in your reading, so make a note of these, naming the source, title of the book, page number, and author's name Such information may enable you later to refer quickly to the book, and is readily to hand when you come, at the end of your essay, to your bibliography, should one be required. There is no short cut to this stage of essay preparation. It does help to be as organised as possible, either inside your head or outside with the help of notes and folders.

When the task is to collect information that is relevant to the subject of the essay, don't stand on ceremony. Any information is valuable: ideas, facts, notions, evidence, notes from tutorials, illustrations, diagrams, notes from library books, textbooks, newspaper cuttings etc. Here any notes you may have made in lectures or jottings from books will become useful but don't turn the essay into a straightforward regurgitation of them! Remember the essay is a good way of *revising, reviewing, and integrating* your material and your understanding.

As you go about collecting information, it might help to keep the following points in mind (again, perhaps on a big piece of paper) to stop you straying too far from the topic:
- What is the main theme or argument which I wish to present and sustain in my essay?
- What are the major questions I want answers to?
- Which books appear likely to help me in my work?
- Where do I locate appropriate sources of information?

Some students find it helps them if they write down in list form all the points they wish to cover. Others find that they prefer to have only the sketchiest outline in their minds, so that they have room for manoeuvre. Whatever method you find suits you best, you should be prepared to be flexible, perhaps to be carried along on a different path because of last minute inspiration.

Planning your essay

Now consider your jottings in more detail. You may find that some, on closer consideration are not relevant, reject them. Irrelevant information is 'waffle'. Arrange the information that remains in order to show a clear line of argument end coherent sequence of thought. This must be related to the question; it's no good being clear and coherent about the wrong subject! There are many ways to present an argument. Try to have a logical flow of information, e.g. maybe you can describe something chronologically or historically, setting points or

events out in a time sequence. Similarly, it is often best to contrast two views by arranging equivalent points 'side-by-side' in the essay. If you have difficulty in getting a satisfactory logical structure to your essays, ask your tutor for feedback and assistance, or try your ideas out on a friend or fellow student. The best way to create a structure for your writing is to make a plan, and if you have followed the instructions in the paragraph above, you will have started to make one.

In essay writing, as in other aspects of studying, making a plan is a *good thing* to do. Don't make this plan in your head, write it down; it may even be worth handing it in to your tutor if you want confirmation that you on the right track. (Always write a plan before you start an essay in an exam, that way if you don't get time to finish the question in the time allotted the examiner can see what you were going to say and will probably give you some marks for that!)

A plan will help you in several ways:
- It helps sort out the main ideas from those that are peripheral.
- It makes sure you don't leave out anything vital.
- It makes sure you don't repeat yourself.
- It helps you to use your time efficiently and not sit for half an hour chewing your pen, waiting for inspiration.
- It helps you sketch out a structure or logical order.

The final plan can be written in single telegram-like phrases and sentences, each one referring to the contents of one paragraph of the finished essay, so the plan should be no longer than one half of a side of A4 paper. You will use the information you have collected and refined in the 'sorting out' period referred to earlier. Organise it into a plan that is a skeleton of your intended essay. Here is a basic three-point plan that can be used in a wide variety of essays:

1. Introduction

a) Comment on the subject of the essay. What do you understand by it? How is it important? etc.

b) Which aspects will you deal with and why? Remember you can't say everything about anything in two or three thousand words.

c) Make it interesting. Tutors are people not essay marking machines. They get bored like everyone else. They usually respond well (sometimes very well, enough even to give you extra marks) to being 'entertained' or engaged in some way.

2. The Main Body

a) Develop your main idea or argument through a number of paragraphs. (Developed on pp.111 - 114) Keeping roughly to the rule 'one idea per paragraph', any more and the essay will seem cluttered and over complicated.

b) Support the main idea within each paragraph with examples and illustrations drawn from experience or other authors, remembering to name your sources, including yourself by saying 'I think', 'In my view' or 'I have found' etc.

3. Conclusion

a) Summarise your main points or ideas, using different words if possible.

b) Comment generally on the topic of the essay indicating wider indications, future trends or scope for further consideration.

Steps towards the plan

Turning the untidy mass of material you have into a neat half page plan is easier said than done, you may need to take steps to get you there. The material needs to be knocked into some sort of shape before you can really see what you've got, and if there are any gaps, and how well it will answer the question.

1. Reduce your collected material to a set of headings and subheadings and either write or scatter them onto a large piece of paper.

2. Look at them for a while to let what you've got sink in and perhaps begin to suggest some pattern or form.

3. You could try cutting them up and rearranging them on the floor into logical groups in a logical order. Divide them into the three large sections of introduction, main body and conclusion as mentioned earlier. (Word processors are great for this, using 'cut' 'copy' and 'paste' commands.)

4. In these groupings or structure, draw connecting lines between them to show how they relate to one another and the order in which they will be written down.

5. Now you are ready to write your final plan.

Having the plan you are now ready to write the essay. However, many students get so far along the path to writing an essay and then falter. Some of us love collecting the information, but we think that we should read just one more book and then... Others plan and plan and never seem to get down to writing that all-important first sentence of the first draft...

Hang-ups about writing

After 18 years of working in further education, I know that the usual staff-room tin-pot psychology explanation for students having difficulties in writing essays is that students are bone idle. I also know that the average counselling course tutor (and student) will have a more sophisticated appreciation of the difficulties that we can all experience in the completion of written assignments.

Most students, on being set an assignment seem able to produce something, even if they know that their work has its imperfections. Some, however, are afraid to commit themselves to paper because what they write is going to be assessed. This difficulty seems to apply most frequently to the essay-type of assignment perhaps because students are, amongst other things, expected to present and to justify their own views, to indulge, in fact, in a particularly dreadful, forced indecent exposure.

Three escape routes commonly taken by such students are:
    (a) asking for an extension of the deadline, giving reasons for not meeting it,
    (b) failing to meet the tutor at an agreed time to discuss progress in the writing of the essay,
    (c) being 'ill'

The point being made here is this: it is not always idleness that prevents students from producing the assignment on time, although obviously it sometimes is. Some of the most conscientious, highly motivated students experience this difficulty.

If you are in this position, you should discuss your difficulty with a member of staff, for example, your own tutor, another tutor you feel may be helpful, the student counsellor, or a tutor from the study skills centre if you are somewhere that has one. It is unwise to allow the difficulty to drag on, so that your life becomes a misery.

Many students at some time or other, when confronted with an essay title, say "I've got nothing to write about". On occasions this may unfortunately be true, and can be due for example, to a student's lack of understanding of the available material, to the unavailability of relevant material, or to inadequate notes.

Some tutors discuss approaches when setting an essay, and such discussions can be useful. Moreover, if you are doubtful about your grasp of the content and structure you can ask your tutor if they will be willing to look at your plan for your essay and tell you if they think you are on the right lines.

Writing the essay

It's at this point in the whole process of essay writing that a number of students simply give up. They've summarised the textbooks, got all the references, read and re-read their lecture notes and yet they still can't set pen to paper. Perhaps this is because there is too much material giving intellectual indigestion. Be ruthless and prune some more if this is the case. They have a real block against writing that crucial first sentence or two. One solution to the problem could be to break down the task into a few basic steps, section by section, paragraph by paragraph, point by point. Instead of seeing the essay as a huge mass, a whole entity, divide it up into smaller units and set yourself the more manageable goal of completing these smaller pieces of writing. Or if it's the written words that are causing you the problem then try speaking your essay into a cassette recorder and transcribing it until you feel confident enough to miss out the recorder

Style

Once you have chosen your essay title, collected the relevant material, made a plan of the contents and their structure you are still left with another thing to think about. What *style* should it be written in?

In everyday life we are offered many different writing styles, you only have to compare the styles of the tabloid and broadsheet newspapers, the language used in estate agents' advertisements for houses is very different from that advertising financial services, the letter you'd write to a friend has a very different style from the information booklet that comes with your tax return. You are faced with a choice to make about what use of language is appropriate for your written assignment.

Obviously the best thing to do would be to check with your tutor as to what is expected. But the options are likely to be:

• *academic* - written in the formal language used by academics, a rather brief, precise style where there is little or no room for personal anecdotes or feelings.

• *journalistic* - written in the more informal style of a newspaper, the language is less stilted and more expressive and colourful.

• *chatty/colloquial* - much closer resemblance to how we speak naturally to friends and others who we are not trying to impress, with all the slang and relaxed language of home or street. This will contain much use of anecdote and personal opinion.

• *narrative* - rather like telling a story, often from your own point of view. This is a useful style when describing your own experience, as you may be asked to do in counselling essays.

To some extent the style will be dictated by the purpose and the nature of the material. It would be no good being chatty and anecdotal when asked to compare and contrast Behavioural and Person-Centred Therapies for example. Conversely writing in an academic style about your counselling practice wouldn't be appropriate either.

If, having asked your tutor, they are happy to leave the choice of style up to you then think about doing something either that you'd enjoy or that you'd feel safe with. Play around with some ideas, as long as you answer the question, it could be fun, and the chances are that if you've enjoyed writing it then it will also be good to read. (See box on pp 124 - 125 for an illustration.) **Note:** Always aim to say what you have to say in as few words as possible; tutors appreciate brevity and the number of marks you get will decrease rather than increase with length. Remember that verbose or over-elaborate language does nobody any favours, it usually only clouds the issue and makes the writing appear stilted and unnatural. Even the most complicated and profound ideas can be expressed in clear, simple language; counselling ideas should be accessible to all no matter what their academic or social background and obscuring the voice of counselling excludes rather than includes others.

Using your plan to write a first draft

Following the outline of your plan and using the information below to expand the three main areas of the essay write a first draft in rough to see how the whole piece looks. You may be getting impatient at this stage but your patience will be rewarded when the marks are allocated! The draft is a longer, fleshed-out version of the plan and will contain the three main areas as mentioned earlier - the Introduction, Main Body and Conclusion.

Introduction

This, although it is the logical place to start, is sometimes the most difficult place to begin writing. Because the introduction is usually the first thing to greet the reader, look at it as just that - a first meeting. (We all know that first impressions can make a difference as to how the rest of the 'relationship' goes.) In order to encourage the reader to continue the introduction needs to do two things; it needs to grab their attention and to tell them what to expect in the rest of the piece. If you just can't get to grips

with this tall order before you start writing leave it until you feel you can write something that will get your writing off to a good start. It may not be until you have finished the whole essay that you can come up with a good Introduction, particularly if your essay has taken on a life of its own and you find your writing has developed an unexpected slant during the writing process.

Main body

Many students fail to see the necessity of a logical progression to this largest and most important part of their essay, they simply write down lists of points as the ideas occur to them. The plan is the first line of defence against this. The second is working out a logical progression of ideas for your essay that is related to the title or question set. It is very frustrating reading ideas that seem to appear out of the blue with no connection to what has come before or link to what follows. Ideas, points, paragraphs and sentences need to flow logically and clearly from one to the other. Imagine going to the cinema to see a film where the scenes were all jumbled up; nothing would really make any sense. You would get some idea of what it was about but it would be a very unsatisfactory experience and you'd come out of the cinema being non the wiser. And in the case of the tutor marking a jumbled essay they would probably think that the student was non the wiser too!

Here are some ways of organising your material remembering that it must always relate to the question.

1. Story telling. The easiest structure is the one that naturally flows from the telling of a story or the recounting of events e.g. in an essay giving the history of the development of a theory or therapeutic approach or explaining some personal event.

2. Cause and effect. This also suggests a logical structure. You describe the cause of something then explain the effect it's had.

3. Before and after. This is the describing of a situation or event before something happens to it then you would explain how it's different after something has happened to it, e.g. the behaviour of young people regarding being offered drugs before they have had a programme of education and after that programme.

4. For the argument and against the argument. Again this type of essay carries its own inherent structure. You would put forward the case for example for counselling as a means of helping people in distress and then you would just as impartially put the case against 'the talking cure'.

Remembering all the time to limit yourself to one aspect of the answer per paragraph and one idea, or point per sentence.

Conclusion

This gives your essay a rounded-off feeling, a feeling that it has come to a natural end. It is also an opportunity to summarise the main point of your essay and to leave the reader with a clear understanding of what you have been saying and perhaps pointing to further areas of study in the future. Again like the Introduction it may be better for you not to leave the conclusion to the end but to write it near the beginning to give you something to aim at, so that you know

exactly where you are going. But beware, it may have to be re-written if you find that you ideas change and develop during the course of writing.

Having written your first draft

Now have a critical look at your work thus far (even better, get someone else to have a look at it to check spelling and see if it 'hangs together'.)
Use the following checklist:

• Does the essay answer the question or deal with the topic set?
• Does it cover the main aspects in sufficient, but not too much, depth?
• Is the material logically arranged?
• Is each main point well supported by examples and/or argument?
• Is there a clear distinction between your ideas and those you have brought in from other authors?
• Is the essay the right length for its purpose? Essays that are too long may be marked down (and can be taxing for the reader).
• Is the language clear and is the style suited to the purpose?

Being satisfied that you can answer 'Yes' to the above questions you are ready to start the final version of your essay. You know what the question is asking, what you are going to write and in what order. There are still some points to bear in mind though as you begin writing. Remember that studying is about *communication,* whatever you are learning will be communicating something to you, your job in assessments is communicating what you have learned to your assessor. You are writing the essay for a purpose, and you must make sure it fulfils that purpose and the purpose is usually to demonstrate not only that you know something about the topic in question but also that you can express what you know in a clear coherent way. It's of little use knowing something if you can't out it into words in ways that others can understand.

Presentation

You expect your work to be read by at least one other person so try and make the reading of your work a pleasant and enjoyable activity. It is always nicer to read a neatly written, grammatical, properly punctuated essay with correct spelling. Your essay will create a better impression if you follow these simple suggestions:

- Check out the requirements for presentation, e.g. single sided paper, double/single spacing etc.
- Type or word-process you essay if at all possible.
- If you can't type it, use the same size paper

Plagiarism and the use of quotations

Plagiarism

In all "Aids to Study" booklets concerned with note-taking from books and lectures you are advised to take notes in your own words. Rephrasing a lecturer's or author's expressions will help you to understand the meaning and learn the idea more effectively. It will also help you to avoid the serious offence of plagiarism when you come to use your notes to construct an essay. Basically plagiarism in this context consists of attempting to pass off other people's language, sentences, words or ideas as your own. Naturally, you need to make extensive use of other people's work in writing your essay. But this has to be done in an acceptable way. At times you may think that an author has expressed a point you wish to make in a particularly clear, concise way. In this case direct quotation and acknowledgement is called for.

Using quotes

If, for example, you wanted to make a direct quote from the preceding paragraph, but not the whole paragraph, you would put inverted commas (either double " or single ') around the chosen words, and indicating by a series of dots thus .... that some words have been missed out if they did not serve your purpose as follows:

When trying to remember '... *from books and lectures you are advised to take notes in your own words. Rephrasing a lecturer's or author's expressions will help you to understand the meaning and learn the idea more effectively. It will also help you to avoid the serious offence of plagiarism ... Basically plagiarism in this context consists of attempting to pass off other people's language, sentences, words or ideas as your own. Naturally, you need to make extensive use of other people's work in writing your essay. But this has to be done in an acceptable way... In this case direct quotation and acknowledgement is called for.'* Sanders (1995 p.100)

(A4) and the same colour ink (preferably black or dark blue for readability) throughout.
• Write the question out in full at the top of the first page and any assignment code.
• Leave a generous margin, this allows the reader to make useful comments in this space.
• Number each page.
• If you can afford it, write on one side of the paper only.
• Remember to include your name and the course you are following!

Note: When it comes to the appearance of your work a typewriter is useful but access to a word processor is even better. Plans become drafts and drafts become the final essay much quicker with the help of a word processor. If you have access to one but are unsure or nervous about using it try to get someone to help you build confidence, they are a wonderful aid for any student.

Reviewing the essay after completion is an important but sometimes neglected step. Reviewing requires resisting the temptation to put the essay aside in your relief at having finished, and not to handle it again until it is submitted to the assessing tutor. But it can be argued with some Justification that an essay has not been completed until it has been reviewed. Reviewing entails reading the essay again, trying to distance yourself from it, putting yourself in the place of an outside observer, being constructively critical. It is sometimes found that the most effective time to review an essay is a day or two after it has been written, because you come back to it and see it as if with new eyes. Unfortunately these new eyes don't always like what they see and we are sometimes over

critical of our own work so try hard to be objective.

Another salutary experience can be had by getting a colleague to read your essay and to comment on it before you present it for assessment. A second person can often find flaws that you yourself missed, and they can also be a great boost to the confidence that has shrunk because you are too close to the essay to be able to see its good points.

One excellent way to check that your essay flows and that the sentences actually make sense and that the words actually say what you want them to say is to read it aloud to yourself listening carefully to what you are saying. Better still read it aloud to someone else, whilst still listening yourself because you know what you are supposed to be saying and a listener will not be as familiar with the content as you are.

Revising the essay in the light of your own review could be the final step before it is presented for assessment. Revising does not necessarily mean the large sections should be re-written, but more often that minor adjustments would improve it.

Note: Always get at least one photocopy of it before handing it to your tutor for final assessment; it is not unheard of for essays to be left on trains or to disappear down the 'black hole' of the tutor's 'filing system'.

Bibliography and References
Basically a bibliography is a list, in alphabetical order, of all the books you have used in writing your essay. (You'll see now why it is particularly useful to keep a note of these as you go along.) The list includes any books you have used to inform your thinking and writing, or have used as sources of inspiration. Whereas the references are a list, again in alphabetical

Model Answer 4: *Essay (2500 words)*

ARE THE 'CORE CONDITIONS' PROPOSED BY CARL ROGERS BOTH NECESSARY AND SUFFICIENT?

Tutor's comments

In Rogers' book "On Becoming a Person" he states his overall hypothesis: '...if I can provide a certain type of relationship, the other person will discover within himself the capacity to use that relationship for growth, and change and personal development will occur .'

A good quote to start with, but you really should have put the date in and the page number.

Writing in 1957, Rogers proposed that there are six conditions necessary for constructive personality change. These are : -

1. That the two persons are in psychological contact. That is that they both understand what they each are to do in the relationship, that they are both 'on the same wavelength'.
2. The client is in a state of incongruence, being vulnerable or anxious.   By incongruence Rogers means that the client is out of touch with his true feelings, that his perception of himself is distorted.
3. The therapist is congruent in the relationship or integrated in the relationship. This means that the therapist needs to be genuine and not present a facade to the client. Rogers felt that the only way that the client can find the reality in himself was through the reality in the relationship with the counsellor.
4. The therapist experiences an unconditional positive regard for the client. This means an acceptance of and a regard for his attitudes of the moment. The counsellor must see the client as having a worth and dignity in his own right. It is this positive regard that makes the relationship warm for the client and, Rogers argued, this safety of being liked is highly important in the helping relationship.
5. The therapist experiences an empathic understanding of the client's internal frame of reference and endeavours to communicate this to the client. Rogers gave this empathic understanding a greater prominence in his later writings. He believed that the person reacts to the field as he experiences it and this perception is reality to that person. Consequently, the best vantage point for understanding behaviour is from the internal frame of reference of the individual himself. That is, using their perceptions of events.
6. The communication to the client of the therapist's empathic understanding and unconditional positive regard is to a minimal degree achieved.

You have not made it clear whether these are your words or Rogers' words, or which is which. Remember to put the page numbers in for any quotes as well. Otherwise this introduction is well explained, clear and as brief as you could make it given the nature of the six conditions.

Are you sure 'liked' is the right word here? Look at what Dave Mearns has to say in 'Developing Person-Centred Counselling'.

I know Rogers uses this term in 'Client Centred Therapy', but I think you should explain it here.

You might consider including "...as the locus of their 'reality'", here to make this clearer.

Model Answer 4: Essay (continued)

Tutor's comments

It is through satisfactory provision of these conditions that Rogers says the correct climate for personal growth and development will occur. The third, fourth, and fifth conditions are regarded as the 'core conditions'. Rogers argued that these conditions are both necessary and sufficient for desirable change to occur in clients, and he believed that these conditions are present in all types of effective therapy. He claimed that if one or more of the conditions is not present constructive personality change will not occur. He believed that the treatment technique is not an "essential condition of the therapy". Techniques merely serve as channels for fulfilling one of the conditions. He displays consistency in his theory and acknowledges that his own form of therapy is convenient but not essential - "this technique (client centred) is by no means an essential condition of therapy".

If you want to give your work more authority, you could use a word like 'asserts' instead of 'says'.

This bit isn't clear - what are you actually trying to say? Perhaps you could try putting it a little more simply or an example might help.
A reference here would help.

"The more that the client perceives the therapist as real or genuine, as empathic, as having unconditional regard for him, the more the client will move away from the static, fixed, unfeeling, impersonal type of functioning, and the more he will move towards a way of functioning marked by a fluid, changing acceptant experiencing of differentiated personal feelings. The consequence of this movement is an alteration in personality and behaviour in the direction of psychic health and maturity, and more realistic relationships to self, others, and the environment". (Rogers 1967 - p.66).

I'm not sure I understand fully why you have chosen to include this quote here. Isn't it saying what you (and he) have already said?

Rogers' ideas have generated a lot of research over the years especially into his conditions for constructive personality change and more specifically into those conditions he calls the core conditions of genuineness, empathy and unconditional positive regard. The assertion that these conditions are "necessary and sufficient" is in dispute. Rogers even went so far as to say that these conditions were requirements for all techniques of psychotherapy not just his approach, a view that has also been expressed by Truax & Carkhuff (1967). Halkides in 1958 performed a study taking a sample of 20 client/therapist pairs and had them judged by three judges who rated them for the level of the therapist's rating on the three core conditions. He found on the basis of the greatest amount of client improvement that there was the greatest improvement in the clients whose therapist had scored well, in the judges opinion, in the satisfying of the three core conditions. However, this study does not say if all three conditions are always required. For example, is it always necessary for the therapist to be congruent if he is still empathic and still has positive regard for the client?

This is a good, clear summary of the research. It is also good evidence of wide reading for the essay. How did you come across these papers - did you get them from the library? Well done!

Sorry to be picky, but there should be an apostrophe after judges'.

Model Answer 4: Essay (continued)

Truax and Carkhuff (1967) devised a set of scales to measure the degrees of accurate empathy, non-possessive warmth and genuineness in their assessment of the importance of these factors. Their scales were developed using audio-tapes of the interviews to assess the success of the counsellor in communicating the three 'core conditions'. The authors did not listen to all of the taped recording of every session and therefore may have taken the samples out of context. This would shed some doubt on their conclusions. It is also questionable if audio-tape is the best medium for this sort of research.

Such a method of assessment would not be able to take account of the effect of posture and facial expressions of the counsellor, the "body language" which is now recognised to be so important in interpersonal relationships. The opinions of the clients as to whether the counsellor had met the conditions was not canvassed nor was the clients opinion of the usefulness of the sessions or their success. This to Rogers would be the true measure of the success of a client based approach. He was quite adamant that it was the client's perception of the communication of the three core conditions that was important. To this end the imposition of a third person without reference to the client would invalidate the trials.

You have a tendency to over-use inverted commas. There is no need to put phrases like this in "quotes".

Gurman (1977) did try to assess the perceptions of the client using the Barrett-Lennard Relationship Inventory which was developed to assess individual psychotherapy. Gurman's results concluded that "there exists substantial if not overwhelming evidence in support of the hypothesised relationship between patient perceived therapeutic conditions and outcome in individual psychotherapy and counselling". However, Gurman's study was the result of only 26 individual therapy studies which raises questions about the validity of the study. Most trials have used sampling methods taking sections of the session and judging. The question must be - are the highest levels of satisfaction of the core conditions necessary through the whole of the session or are certain aspects more important at some times than others?

This is a good critique. I was thinking to myself 'Why do you think this is questionable? Please explain.' But then you did!

Page number missing for the quote.

Many writers have supported Rogers assertions of the importance of the need for the three core conditions but fall short of confirming them to be "sufficient" for constructive personality change. Carkhuff (1966) and Egan (1975) have argued that although the core conditions are necessary they are not sufficient to help the full range of clients who come for counselling. Egan believes that these conditions

No need for the quotes here either, you have made your point that you think the term is questionable.

Model Answer 4: Essay (continued)

and the techniques described are only one stage in the process of bringing about constructive change. Other conditions needed include confrontation, counsellor self-disclosure, alternative frames of reference and problem-solving programmes.

Some critics of the person-centred approach have suggested that there is sometimes no need for any interpersonal relationship at all. Ellis (1975) has reported that personality change does occur without psychological contact with another, through incidences of clients improving simply by reading literature which he calls bibliotherapy. He also claims that he has seen clients helped by therapists who were emotionally disturbed and incongruent. Automated treatments without the presence of a therapist can also be effective.

Lockhart (1984) in the conclusion to his review states that all that can be claimed at present is that a modest relationship exists between the facilitative conditions and therapy outcome. The conditions are indeed helpful but perhaps not "necessary and sufficient". In their introduction to 'Client-Centered Therapy and the Person Centered Approach' (Eds. Levant & Shlien, 1984) show that there was considerable support for Rogers' hypotheses until the mid 1970's, but by the end of the 1970's this was much in dispute as researchers from traditions other than the client-centred tradition conducted studies and exposed faulty research design in previous studies. Levant & Shlien conclude that as far as client centred therapy is concerned neither research methodology nor outcome evaluation have much to be proud of. Later in the book however Neill Watson in a detailed review of a large number of research studies presents a further reflection. He concludes that in his review he found no studies which adequately tested Rogers' hypotheses. Watson ends his review "After 25 years of research on Rogers' hypotheses, there is not yet research of the rigor required for drawing conclusions about the validity of this important theory". (Watson, 1984: 40).

What we fail to realise is that the difficulty that arises from the "necessary and sufficient" hypotheses is because these are "research hypotheses". It is self-evident that we could all think of individual exceptions where one of the 'core conditions' was not necessary and all taken together were insufficient. Rogers sought, in presenting these hypotheses, to encourage the development of theory and research within psychotherapy and to bring into question many of the specious assumptions

Tutor's comments

I know punctuation isn't central to your learning on this course, but some commas would make this much easier to read. I had to go over it a couple of times to get the sense.

I may be me being thick, but you'll have to explain 'automated treatments' - the mind boggles!

Are these Lockhart's words or yours? You must make this clearer - it reads as though they're his. All that's missing are some inverted commas, a date and a page number.

You really have done a good job on the research evidence. Especially considering the essay only asks for 2500 words. You make good points very clearly You have captured the dilemmas and deficiencies inherent in trying to study relationships by counting and measuring things. Research design is very important.

Model Answer 4: Essay (continued)

which existed in psychotherapeutic practice up to that time, e.g. assumptions about the necessity of assessments, treatments, and the therapist being the "expert" who imposed their diagnosis on the client.

In 1986 Rogers stated categorically 'what we need most is solid research'. Throughout his life Rogers never doubted for a moment that psychotherapy needed research backing if it was to develop its effectiveness. This is not to say that researchers have now succeeded in discovering perfect investigative methods but research findings are now more likely than ever before to affect training programmes and clinical practice across many different therapeutic orientations.

I do not have any difficulty with the "sufficiency" hypotheses. When the core conditions exist it would be difficult to conceive many cases where 'constructive personality change' would not take place. There could, however, be frequent occasions when these conditions are not 'necessary' for constructive personality change to occur. For example, many clients come into counselling at a time in their life when things are bad and they are really down. In these circumstances there is possibly a greater likelihood of the client moving in the direction of progression rather than regression. It could be that the only way is to go up. Even if the counsellor attempted to do absolutely nothing, more would show improvement than deterioration over a period of time. So if we were trying to apply Rogers' conditions to individual cases we would find numerous cases where these conditions were not necessary.

So applying the idea of the necessity of these conditions onto individual clients is decidedly an un-person-centred procedure; before we have even met the client, we are deciding what he or she needs! It is better to use the wisdom provided by theory and research as a general guide to our thinking rather than offering us specific predictions on the individual client.

Having been a client myself in both directive counselling and person-centred counselling, I can honestly say that the directive counselling made me more defensive and withdrawn but where the core conditions were offered I blossomed and was able to become positive and open. Also having become a counsellor myself and seeing the "process" work is a wonderful and fulfilling experience. So in my own experience I have no difficulty with the question of the "necessity and

Tutor's comments

Excellent writing. As you point out, no sensible conclusions can be drawn until the nature of the core conditions is identified. I wonder whether any group of half-a-dozen people would agree? (Given this what do you think about the way we assess skills on the course?) Also, what do you think would constitute 'solid research'?

Yes, this is called 'spontaneous remission'.

Good point!

Great. This is a good piece of personal writing from your own 'voice' and experience.

Model Answer 4: Essay (continued)

sufficiency" of the core conditions. I have appreciated the knowledge and understanding which these hypotheses have brought us in our efforts to 'test' them, although person-centred counsellors might argue that research has never tested properly the "necessity and sufficiency" of the core conditions.

In conclusion I would like to refer to "A Fourth Condition" which Brian Thorne (1992) presents in his book on Carl Rogers. He refers to "presence" as Rogers described it "...when I am at my best, as a group facilitator or a therapist.... when I am closer to my inner, intuitive self, when I am in touch with the unknown in me. ... then simply my *'presence'* 'is releasing and helpful...."(Rogers, 1986, p198). Thorne suggests that if Rogers "would have lived we might well have heard much more of the quality of 'presence' and that both the theory and practice of person-centred therapy might have undergone important revision as a consequence". (Thorne 1992, p40).

Yes, it's a good idea to show the further development of these constructs...where they might be leading.

If we are to avoid the pitfall of ascribing everything we do not know (or yet know) to 'intuition' or 'magic', I consider that rigorous self-awareness and particularly the discipline of appropriate self involvement precedes 'presence', as Rogers describes it. Presence, in this transpersonal, almost mystical sense, arises out of the solid practice of developed counselling skills and self awareness over years of practice. Rogers only started writing about presence after over fifty years of practice. So I disagree with Thorne's reference to this as a fourth condition, since the word 'condition' suggests an element without which therapeutic change will not happen. This fourth condition I would not consider to be necessary and sufficient and could be placed under the third core condition of congruence where your self awareness, self involvement and your presence is needed to help the client find his own reality. It is not so much a 'core condition' as a heightened state where all the other conditions are integrated to a degree where they are present in an intuitive sense - the peak of actual practice.

This is a good, confident end to the essay...

I consider the core conditions are necessary and sufficient. However, when employed by an experienced counsellor they can amount qualitatively to more than the sum of their parts.

...apart from this conclusion which is disappointingly hurried. A bit like an afterthought.

Model Answer 4: Essay (continued)

Tutor's comments

BIBLIOGRAPHY
CARKHUFF R R (1966). Helping and Human Relationships - Volumes 1 and 2. New York: Holt Rinehart and Winston.
EGAN G (1982). The Skilled Helper (2nd Ed.) - California: Brookes/Cole.
ELLIS A and HARPER R (1975). A New Guide to Rational Living. North Hollywood, Cal.: Wilshire.

GURMAN A S (1977). The Patient's Perception of the Therapeutic Relationship in Effective Psychotherapy. A Handbook of Research. Oxford Pergamon.
HALKIDES G (1958). An Investigation of Therapeutic Success as a Function of Four Variables. Unpublished Doctoral Dissertation, University of Chicago.
LEVANT R and SHLIEN J. (Eds) (1984). Client Centered Therapy and the Person Centered Approach. New York: Praeger.
LOCKHART W H (1984). Rogers' 'Necessary and Sufficient Conditions' Revisited. British Journal of Guidance & Counselling. Vol. 12 No.2 July - p113 to p123.
ROGERS C R (1957). Client Centered Therapy. London: Constable.
ROGERS C R (1967). On Becoming a Person. A Therapist's view of psychotherapy. London:Constable.
ROGERS C R (1986). Carl Rogers on the development of the Person-Centered Approach. Person Centered Review, 1(3).
ROGERS C R (1986).   'A client-centered/person centered approach to therapy', in I L Kutash and A Wolf (eds) Psychotherapist's Casebook. San Francisco: Jossey-Bass. pp. 197-208.
THORNE B (1992) CARL Rogers - Key Figures in Counselling and Psychotherapy. London: Sage Publications.
TRUAX C B and CARKHUFF R R (1967). Towards Effective Counselling and Psychotherapy: Training and Practice. New York: Aldine-Atherton.
WATSON N (1984). The empirical status of Rogers' hypotheses of the Necessary and Sufficient Conditions for effective Psychotherapy, in R.F. Levant and J.M. Shlien (Eds), Client Centered Therapy and the Person-Centered Approach. New York: Praeger. pp. 17-40.

You seem to be OK on the references.

Overall this is a confident essay. You write well and can integrate your own experience very well too. I can make nit-picking points to help you improve the style and structure, e.g.. You could adjust your language in places to make it a little more authoritative and you could have tried harder to sharpen up the introduction - even though I know you wanted to get the six conditions in. Be more careful with your quotes and ideas from the work of others.

The content is well argued and you make some good points, but I'm not sure what your conclusion is. You stated it in a very hurried and inelegant way.

You do, however, have a sound grasp of the ideas and this comes through very clearly.

order, of all the books you have quoted from directly or referred to in the text. Some people, however, do not make this distinction and put everything together under the heading 'References'.

When you refer to someone's ideas in the text without quoting from their work, you should include their name and the date of the publication from which the ideas are taken. So in the essay the author writes,

Rogers even went so far as to say that these conditions were requirements for all techniques of psychotherapy not just his approach, a view that has also been expressed by Truax & Carkhuff (1967).

to indicate that Rogers' ideas, which had been dated earlier, were shared by Truax and Carkhuff and published in 1967. In the references section at the end of the essay, the author then gives the full details of the publication in 1967 in which Truax and Carkhuff presented their ideas.

TRUAX C.B. and CARKHUFF R.R. (1967). Towards Effective Counselling and Psychotherapy: Training and Practice. New York: Aldine-Atherton.

If Truax and Carkhuff had published two pieces in 1967 which you wished to refer to, you would indicate one as Truax and Carkhuff (1967a) and the other as Truax and Carkhuff (1967b).

If you are typing or hand-writing your essay, put the title of the book or Journal in inverted commas:

Rogers, C.R. (1951) 'Client-Centered Therapy'. London: Constable.

If you are word processing the essay, you could put the title of the book or Journal in italics:

Rogers, C.R. (1951) *Client-Centered Therapy*. London: Constable.

If you wish to quote someone in your work, you should also include the page number on which the quote occurs either before or after the quote:

*Frankland and Sanders (1995 p.179) state that 'The general principle involved in 'third party helping' is **don't try it**.'*

*Frankland and Sanders (1995) state that 'The general principle involved in 'third party helping' is **don't try it**.' p.179.*

Some courses, especially University courses have particular rules about referencing work, and you will probably be given copies of these at the beginning of your course.

If your writing is for publication you will need to seek permission to use the quotes from the publishers of the extract no matter how short it is. They will also require that you acknowledge their permission to use the quote and will suggest the correct words to use if you ask them.

You can get a good idea of what a references section looks like by turning to the end of any academic book, including this one - see page 160.

Case Studies

The majority of counselling courses feature case studies in the mix of assignments. The term *case study* is a generic one which can mean different things in different settings.

Model Answer 5: *Two very different reading logs*

Look at the extracts from two reading logs below. What do you think about them and how do you feel about them? If the aims of the assignment are to encourage a methodical approach to reading; to keep a record of reactions to counselling-related books read during the course; and to provide a useful record for references, do you feel these have been met? What about the obvious differences in style? What feedback would you give? There are deliberately no tutor comments so that you can take the role of peer assessor to both students and make up your own mind.

Extract from Reading Log No.1

Rogers' Necessary and Sufficient Core Conditions Revisited.
William H Lockhart, BJGC, 2, 12, (1984)
Interesting paper on the whole, using 'research' to show that perhaps the core conditions are necessary and sufficient (although there's a question mark in there).

He proposes that the core conditions can be split into understanding or responsive aspects and initiative conditions such as confrontation, counsellor self-disclosure, immediacy, advanced accurate empathy, alternative frames of reference and elaboration of problem solving approaches. To me some of these smack of expertism and are low in respect and congruence (as I understand it) - without which empathy becomes very hard.
[Jan 95]

Experiences of Counselling in Action
Edited by Dave Mearns & Windy Dryden, Sage 1989
Enjoyable book with some salutary lessons for counsellors about how they are perceived by clients. Good chapters about client and counsellor failure.

Again and again clients state that the way they are treated by the counsellor (the genuineness & lack of facade) is the most important aspect of a therapeutic relationship.
[March 95]

Counselling for Anxiety Problems
Richard Hallam, Sage, 1992
A useful book for nurses to assess anxiety levels/problems. From a Cognitive Behavioural background with directive counselling.

Useful in my job as I do groupwork teaching signs and symptoms of anxiety & physiological causes, which although people find interesting *is not counselling as I know it.*
[October 94. Re-read January 1995]

Counselling Survivors of Childhood Sexual Abuse
Claire Burke Drauker, Sage, 1992
Good definitions/assessment procedures for nurses. Useful for counsellors to be aware of some psychology so as not to be taken aback when the 'usual' symptoms of abuse arise. Again the directive nature of the counselling hit me, although the core conditions were always emphasised. Some useful ideas about where to focus client's emotions, though. I still strongly believe in the model that the client is the expert and will move forward as long as the core conditions are provided. Also, I want to be a generic counsellor and there is no way I would want to learn techniques or strategies for every sort of problem. It would be impossible, and I don't think it would work anyway.
[Dec 94]

Model Answer 5: *Two very different reading logs*

Extract from Reading Log No.2

On Becoming A Person - A Therapist's View of Psychotherapy
Carl Rogers, Constable, 1961
Well, it's not bad but awfully heavy going. I can't say Part 6 was of much interest to me, but I loved his waspish demolition of the behaviourists in Part 7.

Carl Rogers on Personal Power - Inner Strength and its Revolutionary Impact
Carl Rogers, Constable, 1978
I wasn't very impressed by this one - it seemed so evangelical and societal. What impresses me is what he has to say about the individual. I know all this stuff has a place, but it just isn't in my head.

A Way of Being
Carl Rogers, Constable, 1980
That's better. Written when he was a very old man, he seems so relaxed - he no longer seems to feel the need to prove himself and the philosophical rambling is very pleasing to me. It feels like a man who spent most of his life as a professional heretic with his finger up his arse finally could unwind and reveal the gut things going on for him with no need for empiricism.

Counselling for Women
Janet Perry, OUP, 1993
By, it made me political! It opened my eyes to the possibility that when women receive individual counselling it implies that there's something amiss with their individual pathology when much of what's 'wrong with women' is about oppression.

- There may be different expectations of a case study depending upon whether you are on a counselling course or presenting one at a meeting.
- There may also be different expectations if you are doing a case study as part of person-centred training rather than, for example, psychodynamic training, and different again for cognitive therapy training.
- Some courses require long or extended case studies with up to 10,000 words. Other courses ask for very short case studies of between 1-2,000 words. Sometimes courses ask for very short case studies in order to help students practice for the case study requirements of the BAC Counsellor Accreditation Scheme.

Notwithstanding these possible differences, case studies do have a general structure which is outlined below. However, the first rule of successful assignment-writing should be practised here, namely *ask the tutors what the requirements are*. In particular ask if there is a preferred way to structure a case study on your course. For example the BAC explains in its instructions to applicants the purpose and requirements of the case study

'...to demonstrate congruence and consistency between current counselling practice and theoretical orientation. Case study 1 should give an account of the counselling process and case Study 2 should illustrate the way supervision is integrated in the counsellor's practice.'

(BAC 1992)

Steps to successful case study writing

1. Find out what is required
The first step in successful case study writing is the

same as any other assignment - find out the purpose and criteria or requirements.

2. *Identify a suitable case or client.*

This is a crucial stage. You should choose a client or case that will provide material that will in turn help you cover all of the criteria and requirements with ease. For example, BAC ask for two case studies, one to illustrate the *counselling process* and another to illustrate your *use of supervision.* These different aims will lead to different requirements, and different structures. Think about the following factors:

• How long have you been seeing the client?

It is probably not a good idea to select a client that you have seen for only two or three sessions. Even if your favoured model is short-term and solution focused, it would be difficult to present a good case study based on such a short relationship. At the other end of the spectrum, a very long relationship (several months or years), may be difficult to squeeze into a short case study.

• Do you want a current client or a past client?

Most of the time you will be asked to write a case study to illustrate your current ongoing work. Using a client who finished their relationship with you more than, for example, six months ago, may not be representative of your current work.

• My best work ever, or my usual run-of-the-mill work?

Again, most of the time, you will be expected to give an example of your everyday, normal work. Going for 'My Best Client Ever' will prove more difficult than you think.

• Are there likely to be confidentiality or ethical problems?

You should, if at all possible, secure your client's permission before using material associated with them in a case study. It is essential and routine practise that you disguise the identity of the client. Remember that you may identify the client by disclosing some unique features of the 'case' without mentioning the client's name. This is a particular difficulty if you work with clients who have a high public profile, either in your community or nationally. They don't have to be a soap-opera star, just the victim of a crime that has been written about in the local paper.

• What does you supervisor think about your choice?

Your supervisor will be an invaluable source of help in choosing the 'right' client for your case study. Ask them for their advice early on in the process.

3. *Plan your writing.*

If you are unfamiliar with how a case study is laid out, there is a short section on how to structure a case study below. From here on, the task of writing a case study is much the same as writing any other assignment. By now you should be familiar with the pattern...

4. *Write the case study.*

This stage can't be avoided any longer!

5. *'Pre-flight' check.*

This is where you read it through and check for errors. Don't ignore or overlook this stage.

The structure of a case study

As I mentioned above, there is not one single universally agreed structure for case studies in counselling. In particular, the structure of a case study, and even the manner or style of writing, is to some extent governed by the theoretical approach of the counsellor doing the writing. Whilst I will comment upon possible differences as we go on, I will present a generic structure which you will have to adapt for your purposes and your course requirements.

Background information about the client and case. Select from the following items those that are appropriate to include in your case study.

• What is the setting in which you see the client? Private practice, GP surgery, day hospital, home visit?

• What demographic details about the client are salient to the case? Age, gender, sexuality, race, current relationships, where they live, etc?

• Presenting problem and what they want out of counselling - why did the client come to see you and what goals do they have for themselves?

• Referral path? How did they come to be referred to you - did they refer themselves, or were they referred by a GP, social services, a voluntary organisation, etc?

• How many sessions have they had so far, or have they finished in counselling with you?

• How frequently do you see them - more than once a week, weekly, fortnightly, whenever they want, etc?

• What kind of counselling contract do you have with this person - for example, is the counselling time limited, are there any special confidentiality limits, are there any special responsibilities, such as the client staying alcohol-free or you not smoking?

First interview.
This is where what is written may be shaped by the theoretical approach you espouse. It depends upon whether you think that the first interview in counselling is for information collection (and then interpreting this information to help you understand the client) or whether you think the first interview is for you to build a safe, trusting relationship with the client in a non-interpretative way. You may think it is acceptable and appropriate to make observations and give details of:

• The visual appearance of the client (physical characteristics, dress, & general self presentation).

• Your best guess at how intelligent they are (including their speech, the type of job they have, etc.)

• Psychological characteristics, including their insight, how 'psychologically minded' they are, and how motivated they seem to be to want to change.

On the other hand, you may think that such information is either not helpful or positively unhelpful, and choose to limit your comments on the first interview to more specific observations of the client's world and your own self-observations, including:

• The way they told their 'story' - hesitatingly, confidently, etc.

• How they described their feelings, anger, sadness, etc.

• What you felt and thought about them - your initial impressions and how this affected you.

• How well you thought the interview went.

• Anything that got in the way of you forming an

acceptant relationship with the client.

The context and history of the client's problem
Again this area may be affected by your theoretical and practical position. Would you specifically ask the client for any of the following information? If not, would you include any of these details in the case study if the client voluntarily provided the information without prompting from you?
- Have they had counselling previously?
- Have they been treated by their doctor or a psychiatrist for a 'mental illness'?
- Are they taking drugs for a physical condition or 'mental illness'?
- Is there any family history of this sort of problem?
- Do they have a history of substance abuse?
- Have they recently been bereaved or suffered loss (job loss, injury, disability, etc).
- Is there anything in their development as a child which might account for their current problem?

Assessment.
Some counsellors are very keen on assessment and some positively baulk at the very mention of the word. I am sure that we all *assess* the situation we find ourselves in with our client as it develops, whether we like to think so or not. We all have to decide some pretty basic things, for example:
- Do we think counselling will help the client, or do they need another sort of help - a medical doctor, a welfare rights officer, etc?
- More specifically do we think *we* can help *this particular* client?
- If we think we can help this client are there any special circumstances prevailing that we have to

take account of when we think about how to approach therapy with this client?
- If we think we cannot work with this client can we refer them on without them feeling rejected?

The main differences in ways of assessing a client and the issues they are bringing to counselling focus on the frame of reference from which the assessment is being done:
- If you are more person-centred in your practice you will let the client assess the situation from their own world of experience.
- If you are not person-centred you will probably assess the client and their needs from your frame of reference. This will include your estimation of their problem and your formulating treatment strategies to help them.

The counselling process.
This is the meat of the case study and you will allocate more words to this section than any other. Your task is not to simply give a blow-by-blow account of the content of the sessions. You will be required to reflect upon what happened and apply some analysis to the events in terms of your philosophy, theory and practice of counselling. The events in question will be not only what the client said and your responses, but also your thoughts, and feelings that were stimulated by your relationship with the client. As you reflect upon this process you may include:
- How has the client developed, changed or moved in the counselling process in terms of your model, e.g. Carl Rogers (1961) seven stages of process.
- How have you contributed to the therapeutic

Writing English

For some readers, the next couple of pages may seem to be a patronising insult and for others they may be a lifeline. Just because we can make ourselves understood perfectly well by speaking is no guarantee that we can write well. Although your primary learning goal on a counselling course will not be written English, it is undoubtedly a skill which counsellors should have. Imagine having to write a report for a GP or a letter to the Criminal Injuries Compensation Board on behalf of a client. You would have to write with authority and with correct grammar, spelling and punctuation. If your letter was poorly written with spelling mistakes, your credibility as an advocate would be severely damaged, along with your client's interests.

There are rules governing written English that some of us have never had the opportunity (or the need) to learn and it can come as a shock to find this out when we get our first assignment back from a tutor. Sometimes tutors have difficulty in giving good constructive feedback on written English because they are not trained to do so, or they might feel uncertain of the rules themselves (even though they can recognise when the rules are broken). *Just look at the English in this book - it's far from perfect!*

If you think you may need assistance with your written English there is no substitute for attending a basic writing course. These are available at most FE colleges. In addition, you will be able to find several guides to writing good English in your local bookshop, from the simple: *Getting to Grips with Punctuation and Grammar* by Catherine Hilton and Margaret Hyder, published by Letts, to books for the serious writer (if you are writing a dissertation) such as *Chambers Guide to Grammar and Usage.*

In the meantime, I am offering some very rudimentary guidelines in these panels to help you along. If, when reading trough this panel, you find that you really do not know what makes a sentence complete, or what tenses or punctuation to use, or you recognise some of the common errors in writing, I strongly suggest that you get assistance.

Sentences
When we speak, we do not necessarily use sentences. In written English, however, it is essential to use complete sentences. Most of us can 'hear' whether a collection of words is a proper sentence or not We don't have to stop to think about it or try to identify verbs, subjects and objects. It will help, therefore to read your work out loud slowly. If it sounds OK it probably is. If your work sounds 'wrong' when you read it out and you cannot make it sound 'right', get help.

Tenses
The *tense* of a piece of writing refers to its setting in time: past, present or future. The part of the sentence which indicates the tense is the verb.

Writing English continued

Things can happen in the past, present or future. (There are other possibilities, but these are not worth worrying about at this basic level.)

The main point about tenses in writing is that the piece should be as consistent as possible, i.e. in one time frame only, not shifting needlessly between past, present and future. In an academic essay we would try to stay in one tense (usually the present) to avoid too much unnecessary shifting of time frames. Although we might wish to indicate that something in the past has affected something in the present. For example, to suggest that Carl Rogers' writing in 1957 has affected counselling practice today we could write:

In 1957 Carl Rogers described the essential conditions for successful therapy. Many practitioners keep these conditions at the heart of their counselling practice today.

The first sentence is in the past, the second is in the present. As a general rule, try not to shift tenses within a sentence.

Plurals

We should always make singular and plural instances match up, but in spoken English there are so many colloquial and dialect ways of breaking this rule that some people find it almost impossible to keep to the rule. It is incorrect to write:

There was six counselling sessions on the timetable.

Since 'was' is singular and 'counselling sessions' is plural. The sentence should read

There were six counselling sessions on the timetable.

Also there are some words which commonly cause confusion in terms of plurals. Examples which might creep into a counselling essay include:

Singular	Plural
Phenomenon	Phenomena
Criterion	Criteria

A common mistake is to write the plurals of these words in cases where a singular version is required, such as:

Transference is not a valid phenomena in Person-Centred theory and practice.

This is incorrect because *phenomena* is plural and *transference* is singular. It should read:

Transference is not a valid phenomenon in Person-Centred theory and practice.

Punctuation

This is the formal system of written symbols that tells the reader how the grammar in your writing works. Sentences start with capital letters and end with full stops. Commas break up segments of a sentence but are largely over used. They should generally not be used before the words 'but' and 'and'. Commas also break up lists and you can also use semi colons for this purpose.

Writing English continued

Apostrophes

These are *not* related to plurals. An apostrophe indicates either ownership or omission (contraction of a word).

• *Ownership:* A sign that says *'Hamburger's £1.50'* is wrong. The £1.50 does not belong to the hamburger. It should read simply *'Hamburgers £1.50'*. Also when a name ends in an 's', like Rogers for example, it is incorrect to use an apostrophe to separate the 's' from the rest of the word. The man's name is Rogers, so to indicate that the book *On Becoming a Person* is his work, we write: 'Carl Rogers' book *On Becoming a Person*', not 'Carl Roger's book *On Becoming a Person*'. The latter sentence means that a man called Carl Roger wrote a book called *On Becoming a Person*. It is also incorrect to write "Carl Rogers's book...", since it is only proper to put an 'apostrophe s' after a name that doesn't end in an 's'.

• *Ommission:* An apostrophe is put in the place of missing letters when we contact a word, such as *don't* as a contraction of *do not*, or *can't* as a contraction of *can not*.

Common errors in writing
Unnecessary words:
'I myself, personally...' When simply 'I' will do. 'At this moment in time...' Just say 'Now' or 'At this moment'.
Words in the wrong place:
'This client needs counselling badly.' (Which actually means that the client is in need of bad counselling.) Should read *'This client badly needs counselling.'*

Colloquial English or slang

Slang refers to *spoken* words, phrases and grammatical constructions outside standard English. Nowadays, slang words can enter standard English quite quickly, but written English is more strict and it would still be incorrect to write:

• *Your,* meaning 'you are' which should be written as *you're*. (It's a contraction - see apostrophes)
• *'I will learn you'*. (Meaning I will instruct you.) instead of *'I will teach you.'* or
• *'Can I lend the book from you?'* and *'I'll borrow you the book until next week'* instead of *'Can I borrow the book?' 'Yes, I will lend it to you.'*

Split infinitives

There's no need to worry about these any more. Most English scholars agree that written English no longer needs to be governed by rules that only make sense if you are writing in Latin.

Shame

Feeling ashamed because you can't write good English is a common and serious error. Not everyone had the privilege of a grammar school and university education, not everyone's best language is English. Do not be afraid to ask your friend or tutor where you can go for help. If you are afraid to do this ask at your local library.

process in terms of your theory, e.g. have you moved the counselling process through stages (Egan) or provided therapeutic conditions (Person-Centred), etc.

• What was the quality of the relationship between you and your client, e.g. did you make psychological contact with your client? How did this develop throughout the relationship?

• Were there any 'magic moments' or key interventions in the sessions which illustrate a theoretical or practice point?

• Did anything happen which runs counter to your theoretical approach or your expectations?

• Did you make any contributions or interventions that you consider to be mistakes?

• If the relationship has ended how did it end?

Use of supervision.
Throughout your relationship with this client you will have taken your work with them to your supervisor. You should choose a couple of specific issues from your work with this client that you took to supervision, how you worked with this material in supervision and what sort of resolution you achieved:

• What supervision issues stand out from your work with this client?

• How did you work with your supervisor on these issues?

• What did you learn from this supervision?

• Have you changed your practice as a result?

Summary
Finally you may want to draw some general conclusions at the end of the case study, but this isn't necessary if you do not feel it is appropriate or if there are no formal requirements to do so.

Other types of writing

For the nearly all of this chapter I have concentrated on the writing of essays, for the simple reason that they are what are required more than anything else. But that doesn't mean that that is all the writing you will have to do - far from it. No matter what you are writing (even if it's a shopping list) the correct style, structure and words will help fulfil the purpose of any writing. The key issue here is, 'What *is* the appropriate style and structure for each different type of written assignment?'

In Chapter 5 pages 89 - 97 I have given some broad guidance on the format usually required in a range of written assignments, but this is not a comprehensive answer to the question. In some cases it is simply inappropriate for any one person to be too specific or prescriptive, it is a matter of style and taste with a few course requirements thrown in. It is important to preserve and develop your individual creativity in the face of all the forces (including our own fear) which push us towards a rather grey uniformity in our writing. A personal journal is not an academic piece of writing. You would probably not start your personal journal like this:

Personal development is a well-documented strand of counselling training (BAC Code of Ethics and Practice for Trainers). On the current course it is a requirement and since it is necessary to make regular entries, I propose to write something each week following my attendance at the course.

In this personal journal I intend to look at my own experiences in a number of parts of my life. There are precedents for this in less formal writing and diary-keeping, and I hope to stay close to this tradition in my own work here.

In the absence of course requirements that may set limits on style and content, it would be silly (and, in my view, insulting) for me to suggest to *you* how *you* might write *your* personal journal. First find out what the requirements of the assignment are, and how flexible the tutors think the requirements are. Then you will be free to interpret the work in whatever way feels comfortable and appropriate to you. Written assignments can include:

Personal Journals: An informal, personal style is most usual for this kind of assignment. However, some courses collect and assess personal journals so it is worth checking out just how far you can go in determining your own way of doing it. When given a totally free hand, trainees have included drawings, paintings and other expressive non-written pieces of work. I have known others submit tape recordings of speech, poetry, personal drama acted out by themselves, and music. If supported by your course, the facility to use a variety of media in your personal journal to supplement the written material can lead to a much more vibrant record of your learning.

Try following your own instincts when writing your personal journal. You may wish to make regular entries rather like a diary, or you may wish to wait until there is something worth reporting. (Each of these approaches has advantages and disadvantages.) Some prefer to focus on the course and personal learning and development triggered by or associated with it, i.e. what emotional reactions were triggered by watching a video on bereavement or taking part in a workshop on anger.

Remember to check out groundrules and confidentiality with whoever will read your journal as part of the assessment process.

Book reviews: The best way to get an idea of the style and language used in conventional book reviews is to read some. Look in a newspaper or the BAC Journal *Counselling*, for the structure and content. Your course tutors may not want a formal 'academic' review, so make sure you understand the requirements of the assignment before you start.

If you read around a little you will find that reviewers inject a little of themselves into the review. It is not expected that the review is 'objective' or 'neutral'. The reviewer has license to say what they really think. You don't have to say it's a good book just because Carl Rogers wrote it!

The book review on p.92 is a fairly typical example. Book reviews are usually short, so there is some skill in writing concisely - do not get too flowery or descriptive, use long quotes, or concentrate on one aspect of the book too much, otherwise the words will have been eaten up and the finished product unbalanced.

Presentations: Yet other styles of writing are required for presentations:

Firstly if you are presenting a paper it will be quite formal and academic, rather like an essay.

Secondly if it is a more informal workshop

you will need to make notes of 'key points' on cards to prompt your presentation.

Thirdly you will undoubtedly have to make a plan for your presentation unless it is a formal reading of a paper. Take a look at the plan on page 148. Your course tutors may ask you to follow certain headings, but some or all of those on page 148 will be used:

Aims, outline of content, materials used, timetable (a minute-by-minute, blow-by-blow account).

Finally you may well want to issue a handout to your audience or participants at some point. A handout can be many things from a copy of the paper you are reading , to a sheet of bullet-points covering the main issues in the presentation. Most usually you will be writing an educational handout, summarising the main points of your talk with some references at the end. The general rules are as follows:

• Make sure you have a good, clear title which will unambiguously remind the reader of the presentation in the years ahead. Date it and put the course title and training intuition on the top as well, not forgetting your name to help the tutor locate it for assessment.

• Look at course handouts issued by your tutors to get a feel for the style required.

• Keep the points simple and as short as possible.

• A few short quotes will help liven it up.

• Use diagrams if they help explain a point better than words.

Feedback on the work of your peers*:* This can be written feedback on either taped assignments or essays. This is a tricky piece of writing. You have got to do three things with it:
• Be honest.
• Be yourself - not too formal (this would sound too arrogant - as though you were 'playing the tutor'), not too informal (this would sound disrespectful - as though you had not taken the peer assessment seriously).
• Be understandable. Don't disappear into the clouds in esoteric prose. Be clear and to the point, don't waffle - especially if you have something negative to say, say it cleanly and clearly, but not brutally.

Finally remember that written comments last. Consider the work and your feedback very carefully before giving any kind of feedback - written or otherwise. Any comments you make about others may come back to haunt you, since they will, as I have pointed out elsewhere, say as much about you as they say about them.

Dissertations*:* Are extended essays and your essay-writing skills will serve you well. You will have to structure a dissertation differently (e.g. including a literature search, or chapter headings see p.93) and your style may have to become slightly more formal. Your arguments should be very carefully laid out and follow on logically building to your conclusion.

Research proposals and reports*:* Again, the basic skills are the same as essay-writing. You will have to structure the work according to a traditional format (see page 99).

Do not be fooled into thinking there are huge differences in style. If you can research, plan and write an essay, you can do a research report too. The few stylistic points worth bearing in mind are:

• Write 'It is proposed that...' and '...materials will be used' in the proposal and write in the past tense in the report.

• Also write impersonally, as though the research was done by an unknown individual or group, i.e. 'Participants were chosen at random...' and 'It was decided...', and 'The researcher's home was used to interview....'

• Be formal rather than familiar - don't write 'I think...' this or that.

• Use the appropriate research terminology.

• Assume you are writing for an expert reader, you will not have to explain the terms you use.

Therapese - *How to sound like a counsellor without really being one.*

I have been given permission to reveal the interim results of some top-secret research into the use of language in therapy. It will be of use to all counsellor trainees who find themselves lost for words when writing essays, case studies, dissertations and research reports; and let's face it, that means you and me!

What I have permission to reveal (for the first time anywhere) is the Heuristically Engineered Language Processor (or HELP) for therapists; an instrument comprising a word-phrase bank and protocol which can be used to generate phrases, sentences paragraphs and whole papers without any knowledge of counselling theory or practice at all! In linguistic terms it is high in surface structure and low (if not completely) lacking) in deep structure. In lay terms this means that it reads or sounds as though it makes sense, but, and here's the beauty of it, *it means absolutely nothing at all!* Although, of course there is a slight chance that, if you do not follow the instructions carefully, you may construct a meaningful phrase.

The diligent readers amongst you may have spotted that the research team has already piloted the HELP system in some journals and books, although I am not at liberty to say which ones. If the BAC Journal *Counselling* ran a 'Pseud's Corner' style feature, you could be sure that some HELP-generated work would find its way there. The HELP system has wider uses than just generating meaningless academic-style twaddle. It has applications in therapeutic practice in a number of approaches:

In REBT, practitioners use it to execute an ABC double-bluff manoeuvre, since a totally meaningless phrase which sounds as though it has great meaning provides a therapist intervention which sounds rational

but isn't. Many REBT therapists have struggled to implement this double-bluff strategy without much success because they do it the wrong way round - they construct phrases which actually do mean something, but *sound as though they don't.*

Psychodynamic therapists have realised that an apparently meaningful phrase (which is, of course meaningless) is the ideal projective tool in verbal terms. Clients can see any meaning they like in the words and the therapists interpretations are not hampered by any residual *real meaning* in the utterance.

Person-centred counsellors have tried using the HELP system when they can't understand what the client is saying. It is the ideal tool to meet nonsense with nonsense and thus create the perfectly empathic reflection - the Holy Grail for client-centred therapists. The research team actually got the whole HELP idea from person-centred counselling courses since they observed many trainee person-centred counsellors accidentally stumbling upon HELP-style meaning-free phrases by trying to use intuition before they were ready.

And of course, wherever therapists congregate, a sort of 'jargon-fest' ensues in which outsiders can't understand a word. Now using HELP it is easy for counsellors to create a welcoming ambiance in which no-one has a clue what anyone is on about and everyone can feel just as isolated and insecure as everyone else; creating total therapist-outsider power-dynamic equivalence.

To use the system simply select a word or phrase at random from each column A - E in turn (you may have to add in the odd 'the', 'and', 'if' or 'but'), for example: 'boundaried supportive script-work demystifies subpersonality conflict'. This sounds not

A	B	C	D
empathic	cognitive	Reaction-formation	solve(s)
irrational	reciprocal	musturbation	verbalise(s)
defensive	peer-to-peer	personality structures	integrate(s)
flexible	ethnic	interaction	control(s)
person-centred	client-centred	focus	refute(s)
culturally	phobic	balance	fragment(s)
fluid	Freudian	Myers-Briggs Type	heal(s)
post-modern	effective	behaviour	maximise(s)
sensitive	trauma-related	congruence	deploarise(s)
evaluative	supportive	emotions	approve(s)
conguent	integrated	counselling	work(s) with
phobic	judgemental	gestalts	enhance(s)
interpersonal	organismic self	orgasm	ground(s)
rational	eclectic	script-work	reflect(s)
unconditional	neurotic	constructs	de-mystify(ies)
boundaried	group	perspectives	self-actualise(s)
transactional	one-to-one	analysis	suggest(s)
analytical	behavioural	game-playing	accredit(s)
psychodynamic	individual	Truax and Carkhuff Scale	encounter(s)
Rogerian	psycho-somatic	relationship variables	deconstruct(s)
neo-	Jungian	therapeutic alliance	empower(s)

E
the ABC of REBT
transference and counter-transference
research validated findings
outcome-study results
person-centred attitudes
changing face of counselling in the UK
primary healthcare setting

E (cont)
Necessary and sufficient therapeutic conditions
high potential for assessing client progress
negative self-esteem
short-term solution-focused therapy
codes of ethics and practice
purchaser-provider audit trail
subpersonality conflict

only plausible, but downright inspired. In fact you may think this one may actually mean something, but you would be wrong. That's what makes it great Therapese - even the therapists are fooled, so you can use it with impunity in your assignments. Even Carl Rogers or Sigmund Freud would have to be brave to challenge 'Unconditional neurotic personality structures control negative self esteem', so your lecturer wouldn't have the bottle do anything other than give you a merit.

OK, now it's your turn, but be careful; this is a powerful instrument and must be used wisely and with discretion. If you use it in a cavalier fashion you may find that you've accidentally invented a new therapeutic approach.

Hints and Tips 6

1. Don't start at the beginning by writing the introduction. When completing any written assignment, follow these steps:
   • Read and understand the task - become familiar with the words used when setting essays.
   • Collect and organise the material.
   • Make a plan - introduction, middle or main body and conclusion.
   • Stick to one or two main points per paragraph.
   • Edit your writing so that ideas follow a natural progression, leading up to your conclusion.
   • Review the work before you hand it in, checking spelling etc.

2. When writing up skills assessments or other practical work assignments:
   • It will have helped if you made notes at the time, rather than relying on your memory.
   • Find out what format is required, any special sub-headings etc.
   • Write reports the same day as the action-to-be-reported took place whenever possible.
   • Give an account of what happened, then interpret or evaluate it. Don't assume the reader knows what happened unless you are appending a transcript.

3. Be aware of the pitfalls of plagiarism.

4. Follow whatever course rules there might be for identifying references. Always have a references or bibliography section.

5. If you have problems with writing, let your tutors know. They will have some helpful advice to give and if you are, for example, dyslexic, they will let you know what allowances can be made.

6. If you are worried about your written English, or get feedback from tutors or your peers that your writing needs improving, get help from a book or basic literacy class or seek extra tutorial support from college.

Skills and Techniques for Non-Written Assignments

7

It is common in contemporary education and training to have a variety of methods of assessment, and counselling is no exception. As I mentioned in Chapter 3 and Chapter 5, courses which wish to assess a person's practical skills or competencies will have assignments specifically designed to do that. The written component of such assignments is small if not non-existent. In counselling courses the assignments which fall into this non-written category include the following:

- *Tape-recordings of client work*. Not just the making of the tape itself, but also:
    - The self evaluation and peer evaluation components of these assignments require skills and techniques of *evaluation* and *feedback*.
- *Presentations, seminars and workshops.* Here the skills and techniques of *organising and managing time, arranging themes in a logical order, public speaking* and *personal presentation* come to the fore.
- *Case studies*. I've separated this from the previous heading because the audience will be smaller and in addition to the skills mentioned above, I would add some *meeting management* skills.
- *Viva (from* Viva voce*) or oral examination* You are asked to talk one-to-one with an examiner, moderator or tutor about some aspect of the course. On the rare occasions

that this form of assessment is used, you may be asked to give an account of your personal therapy or personal development.

In Chapter 6 I wrote that all writing is a form of communication, and the remainder of this paragraph repeats the same points and is an acknowledgement that it is *always* the case that an assignment involves you communicating your skills, understanding, competence or knowledge to a tutor or assessor. In non-written assignments you do this by displaying, demonstration, acting out, speaking or whatever is required for that particular assignment. The trick is to do this as clearly and efficiently as possible in a way that not only meets the assignments requirements, but that also benefits you too in that you actually learn something from it to be used as part of your professional or personal development.

Remember that 'assessments are not done for their own sake, they are designed to be of use to you in your learning. They are additional learning opportunities, so use them to learn new material, refine or revise your understanding of old material, integrate new and old material or review old material to get a new perspective on it.'

Before we look at the skills associated with non-written assignments, I would like to re-emphasise one point, namely that the prime skill in successful studying and assignment production and, in the case of practical assignments, the execution of them too, is *planning*. This will come as no surprise to you and those that have read any previous chapters in this book may feel that the point is being laboured. I make no apologies, however, since it is the one clear and consistent factor that separates the majority of students gaining good marks, from those gaining average to poor marks. Most of the skills that follow are built around this pivotal activity of planning.

Tape recordings of client work

There are several aspects of such assignments that require attention:

- *Selecting a suitable client and session*
  What will be your basic approach to tape recording client work? Will you tape routinely, i.e. ask for permission to tape every session with several clients, or will you tape selectively, i.e. waiting to tape a particular session with a particular client? On balance I believe it is better to adopt the former strategy if circumstances and resources (you will use a large number of tapes) allow.

  Tape record a range of sessions for assessment or evaluation. If your course allows, select a first interview, some in the 'middle' of a counselling relationship, and one showing your ability to handle an ending.

  When, for a course assessment, you are asked to select a session that demonstrates your skills, do just that. Don't choose a session where you struggled - that one is for supervision or peer evaluation and feedback. Similarly, don't choose one where the client is silent for the majority of the session. Your skills must be *demonstrated*, and you can only do that when a range of interventions is called for. Choose one that shows off your abilities!

- *Equipment and accommodation*
  Making a tape recording isn't just a matter of putting an unobtrusive tape recorder on the floor, switching it on and forgetting it's there. Cassette recorders and rooms have a tendency to interact to produce a brilliant tape of the toilet flushing next door and a faithful record of the roadworks across the street, whilst relegating you and your client to muffled mumblings that sound as though you are both in a biscuit tin three doors away.

  Test the equipment before you use it. Test the equipment before you buy it if at all possible. (Try to get it on a sale or return basis.) Explain what you want to use it for. Don't think that you need to buy the latest hi-tech machines, a new microphone plugged into your old ghetto-blaster might be the best option. The best microphone I have ever come across is the PZM from Tandy, and although they *are* expensive, they will make most old cassette recorders sound like a BBC studio. Take equipment back if it doesn't do what the sales staff said it would.

- *Ethics and consent*
  It is important to continue to seek informed consent from your clients each time you make a tape. Do not seek, nor assume you have *blanket* permission. Always remind clients that they have the option to refuse, and ask

them at the end of each session whether they still feel OK about you using the tape.

Ask confidently, explaining who will hear the tape or read transcripts, explain why you are making the tape (to improve your counselling skills, or to make sure you are performing up to scratch), and explain who the tape belongs to, that the client has access to it and their right to withdraw it at any time.

• *Self evaluation*

Evaluating your own work is difficult enough when it's just a matter of ticking and crossing right and wrong answers. In counselling and counselling skills training, you are asked to assess your performance in terms of some very personal attributes. How *genuine* are you? How *warm* do you sound? Did that response show that you had *listened* and *understood* accurately?

You should be given scales, checklists or other criteria by which to evaluate your own work. This makes the task somewhat easier. It will also help you select segments of the tape to transcribe and illustrate the skills demonstrated. Listening to feedback from tutors and peers also helps you get the measure of your performance.

In addition to evaluating the skills, also try answering the following questions:
• What do I like about my performance?
• What do I dislike about my performance?
• What have I learned from doing this evaluation?
• What learning goals have I identified as a result of listening to this tape?

• What supervision issues have come up for me?

• *Presentation of your work*

How is your tape recorded client work to be presented.? Are you expected to hand it in to a tutor for assessment, or do you have to play it to a group of peers (and tutor)? There will probably be some supportive written material to accompany the tape. If you are presenting your work to a group make sure there are enough transcripts to go around or that the tutor has enough time to photocopy them.

Make sure that the tape is clearly audible on the machine the tutor or class will be using for playback. If there's a problem you may have to try different playback machines or bring in the machine you recorded it on.

Make sure that the tape is wound back (or forward) to the right point to begin the segment you are presenting for assessment. Be careful if you are using tape counter numbers as reference points since they are not the same on all machines.

Be sure to introduce the tape properly. What is the setting - GP practice, college counselling service? What interview number is it? What was the presenting problem and referral path? Make sure that none of the listeners know the client (this can be tricky since the client may not want anyone to know that they are a client) - it is usually better to tell the client the names of the listeners. Give the names and roles of key 'others' mentioned on the tape, i.e. 'Keith is the client's brother'.

• *Peer evaluation*

Many courses expect trainees to develop not only the skills of self-assessment, but of other-assessment as well. The ability to assess or evaluate someone else's skills, attitudes or capabilities is an important part of the counsellor's repertoire. However, it is not just a question of ticking a box marked 'skill present' or 'skill absent'. In counselling, assessing our peers means saying what you think and feel about a person's qualities. Are they warm? Do they listen well? Are they genuine? Would you, honestly, go to them if you were looking for a counsellor?

Peer assessment is also complicated by the tendency to worry about the reciprocity of the assessment relationship. If I say something negative about them, even if I honestly feel it, will they fail me out of revenge? What will I do when I am expected to assess this person that I have become very close to over the duration of the course? Will I have the strength to tell them what only their best friend should?

On the facing page is a student account of peer and self-assessment. The conclusion is that careful consideration plus honesty is the best way. Treating other peoples work as a precious gift to be respected and treated as if it were your own is a good starting point.

Do not shirk the responsibility of the peer assessor, if you think something is not good enough, say so. Examine your own feelings and motives very carefully. Would you want to have a piece of work passed out of pity or because the assessor didn't have the bottle to be honest? Would you want to be denied the opportunity of learning from poor work and becoming more skilful, or would you rather live under the misconception that you were doing OK really?

Feedback is the key to peer assessment. Being able to both give it and receive it (see page 120) with openness and generosity of spirit is a quality worth developing. The giving of feedback can be facilitated by using a simple rule. In *Next Steps in Counselling (Frankland and Sanders 1995)* I wrote 'In a recent conversation Alan showed me the following *feedback hieroglyph* a sort of picture or symbol which explains how to give good feedback. It's a graphic reminder of a good way of making sure our feedback is balanced and therefore easier to take in.

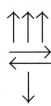

The arrows mean that you make:
• **three** positive comments or things that you like or appreciate about the person's skills,
• **two** alternative ways of trying something, or ways to do things differently, and
• **one** negative comment; a *'I didn't like this bit,'* or *'Don't do that.'*

Presentations, seminars and workshops

Giving a presentation to the rest of the course group on a counselling-related topic is a common feature of many

Inside Story 5: *The Student*
Trials and joys of self and peer-assessment on a diploma course.
Lynn Myint-Maung

Giving and receiving feedback on tapes and essays as part of the assessment was one of the high points on my diploma course. It was an opportunity to see the core conditions in action and improved my embryonic ability to counsel tremendously.

At the beginning of my course, I had no idea what it entailed, just as a new client has little idea of what a counselling relationship will be like. I remember clearly the initial feeling of ignorance and trepidation, and drawing on that every time I met a new client gives me a sensibility about creating a safe environment for that risky time. Not a soft place, but an arena built on foundations of mutual honesty and integrity, so that trust will follow.

That was what happened to me from day one, so that it became a pleasure rather than a risk to bring a particularly naff tape for evaluation. Everyone would share in my embarrassment at the gaffs I made and learn as a result. We could laugh without malice at things which, when I heard them alone, made me cringe, and I could learn then let go of them and move on.

Essays, I guess, were different and yet the same. Different in that a tape involves spur of the moment decisions about how to respond and involves another person. Same in that a great deal of oneself goes into an essay, it represents one's final responses and exposes the considered inner core of self. I noted that people handled one another's essays with reverence and the feedback I gave and received was with one exception, careful and involved a great deal of thought.

The wet kipper I felt I received was a handwritten note on a small piece of paper which gave me a tip on how to do better. I may be distorting how bad this actually was because I felt hurt and because I don't want to be fair about it, I want to tell you how ghastly it felt. Once again I take from this, and recite like a catechism, that I can never afford to be sloppy, or impatient when working with a client. Excuses about feeling ill or upset about something in my own life aren't good enough.

I learned from the giving and receiving of evaluative feedback, that every word, every gesture and pause has weight at this time, just as it does in counselling. That I could not imagine how what I gave would be received, so there was no point in trying to be safe or subtle. The only way for me was to give what I wanted to receive myself; feelings straight from the heart, from the guts. To accept that this was someone doing the absolute best they could, accepting that this was where they were up to. Being prepared to accept anger and bitterness when someone felt disappointed, maybe at failing an assessment, and learning not to take this personally. Just like counselling really.

Giving and receiving constructive and effective feedback

Feedback is the life-blood of counselling training. Both tutors and peers are continually giving feedback to us on a number of levels about a number of facets of our selves. In order to make the best use of this potential goldmine of information, firstly we have to be in a fit state to receive it effectively and secondly the feedback needs to be constructive.

Receiving feedback

• Feedback might be uncomfortable to receive for any number of reasons, e.g:
  • It might be negative, and we don't want to look at the possibility that there are some things that could be improved.
  • It might be positive, and we could have problems handling praise about the good bit of ourselves and our behaviour.

• Listen to the feedback very carefully. If you feel knocked off balance by some of the feedback, check what is being said - have you heard it correctly, and what is meant by the feedback?

• Don't immediately argue with it, or interrupt the speaker to get your defence in before you've heard it all. Try to stay open until the speaker has finished.

• Although it can be useful to check it out with others, don't let it turn into 'Five say I'm warm and three say I'm cold, so I must be warm'. *All* feedback is useful, is saying something about you worth hearing and needs attending to. It's not a matter of the majority votes cast.

• If the feedback isn't what you want or is restricted to one aspect of you, ask for more, or the bits that are missing.

• Decide what you will do as a result of hearing the feedback. Don't just ignore it or put it to one side. Ask others for help if you're not sure how to use the feedback.

Giving feedback

• Think about what you want to say in advance, choose your words and be as clear as you can. Don't 'shoot from the hip' if you can help it.

• Be specific - avoid general comments.

• Own your observations - speak for yourself and not others; say 'I have felt upset by what you've said' not 'It's been an upsetting afternoon.'

• Comment on behaviours that can be changed, not things that the receiver has no control, like lack of hair or a squint.

• Make observations rather than inferences, i.e. 'You were shouting and I noticed Helen cringe', not 'You were obviously into your aggressive father figure there and poor Helen was in the victim role again.'

• Where possible, offer alternatives and leave the recipient with a choice whether to act on the feedback or not.

• Finally, remember that whatever you choose to say about someone else will invariably say as much about you as it does about them. Be mindful, respectful and above all considerate. It doesn't pay to either stab someone in the front with unnecessarily negative feedback or rescue them with inappropriate positive feedback.

counselling training courses. An equally common experience of those confronted with this task is to be variously overawed, overwhelmed, panicked, or blocked. For some of us it might be the first time we have spoken in public or given any kind of verbal presentation. The ability to organise and prepare material, getting ideas into a logical order and presenting them in a memorable fashion are necessary skills for counsellors to acquire. It is important that counsellors and counselling skills practitioners are able to give a good account of counselling theory and practice. Sometimes we might have to give a presentation to other members of a team, managers or a group of volunteers.

Course requirements come in a few different forms. You may be expected, for example, to:

• *Give a seminar or lecture:*

These are quite formal academic events. Often they are an opportunity for the presenter to read a prepared paper, rather than 'shoot from the hip' so-to-speak. If you are asked to give a lecture, it is almost certainly best to write down everything you wish to say and be ready to read it out word-for-word. Getting it typed up in large type, double spaced will help you read it more easily. Remember to leave time for questions at the end.

• *Make a presentation:*

Less formal than a lecture or seminar and possibly less academic. You could be asked to make a presentation on some aspect of your personal experience, for example. You can interact with the audience more than in a lecture or seminar. You may feel comfortable having some parts of the presentation where

you speak more naturally or 'off-the-cuff'. Don't be afraid to use audio-visual aids such as sound bites on tape, films, videos, overhead projector transparencies, flipcharts for interactive exchanges with the audience, etc. You may prefer to take questions at any time during a presentation, or ask people to save them until you have finished.

• *Run a workshop:*

More experiential still, a workshop is an interactive learning experience for participants. A mixture of methods is best, some input, some discussion, some exercises or games, it's up to you to decide on the most appropriate format. You must be prepared for participants to contribute their own personal experiences which might mean that the content gets dragged away from the theme you had planned. Also, participants may experience strong feelings during exercises and games, so make sure you are prepared to facilitate this - your counselling skills will be a good starting point.

The following suggestions are made to help survive the ordeal of giving presentations in general:

• Expect to be nervous, even seasoned public speakers get anxious beforehand. If you've never done it before, finding your 'voice' will take a little practice so do just that - practise with a course member, friend or relative to give you feedback. Also, you will get to hear your own voice, which just as when you hear your voice on a tape for the first time, can sound a little strange.

• If you are worried that you will not be heard,

ask if you're speaking loudly enough.

• Have a plan (see page 148). Stick to it, especially if you're making a joint presentation with a fellow student. The planning process could be similar to that recommended for writing an essay. Adapt it where necessary and if you're working in a pair or team make sure that everyone has had the chance to make an active contribution. Don't let one person do all the research so that they can be excused having to say something!

• Keep it simple. That is to say, don't get too ambitious. You will almost certainly plan to cover much too much material. Also, you will probably overestimate people's ability to pay attention and follow the logical progression of your ideas. Make your points simple.

• Use examples to illustrate your points.

• Vary the presentation by altering your tone of voice, read quotes, show charts or illustrations etc. wherever possible.

• Time yourself - you will get into trouble if you do not read or run through what you plan to say or do at least once beforehand with an eye on the clock. Having too much or too little to say might be awkward.

• Always have some 'gap-fillers' or some extra material in case you get through the planned material quicker on the day.

• Decide whether you are going to read everything or work from cue-cards. Cue-cards are small index-file cards with the key points written large and clear.

• Leave time for questions or discussion. This can be tricky but once the time is used up, move on. Don't run out of time.

Giving presentations can be a great experience and, when you've got over the shock, you may even find it enjoyable. Performing is a great buzz for many people and you might be someone who gets high on it! Remember that this activity is intended to be a learning opportunity for you, a moment of assessment of your performance and capabilities, and finally it is a chance for your audience to learn. Never forget the last of these objectives. Do not distort the learning environment of the group just so that you can put on a fancy show.

Case study or presentation

Case studies are often presented in small groups and unlike medium to large group presentations, the skills involved might include committee meeting, or small group management skills. As far as the preparation of a case study goes, it is as well to bear in mind all of the points made under *Presentations* above and many of the points made under *Tape recordings of client work*, particularly selection of session, ethical issues and presentation of your work.

Bear in mind that it is not so much the content of the case that is being assessed, but your ability to select an interesting case and present it well. You might choose to select a particularly difficult case for example, or maybe one in which you have struggled to perform to you usual standard. Presenting your work for professional scrutiny is a useful learning experience for counsellors and counselling skills practitioners.

In addition you will, as the presenter of a case study, have to manage the time in the meeting. This will involve limiting discussion, making sure everyone has an opportunity to speak and keeping the discussion on track. You may well have to ensure that discussion of client material is kept within ethical boundaries as far as respectful treatment of confidential material is concerned.

The written component of a case study is also important. Make sure that there are sufficient copies of supporting material to go round. Also make sure that all copies of confidential material are collected in and disposed of appropriately.

In real life, case presentations are often a 'team' event, where an interdisciplinary group of helpers get together to understand how they might improve client care. This can be a challenging forum for counsellors where they have to ensure that their relationship with the client is not compromised. Be sure to explain any case presentations to your client and seek informed and ongoing consent. A case presentation during training is excellent preparation for such work in primary healthcare or student counselling.

Viva or oral examination

This method of assessment is not common in counselling training, as I explained in the introduction to this chapter. However, on those occasions when it is used, it has a tendency to strike terror into the hearts of otherwise quite robust trainees. You may be asked to sit a viva if you have missed other crucial assessments because of illness or if your other assessments are borderline. In either case, it is a rare occurrence and hardly worth worrying about or preparing for on the off-chance! You will, though, need to put in some serious preparation if you find yourself having to attend for one.

As with all forms of assessment, planning is the key, so in my list of suggestions to improve your chances, you will not be surprised to see preparation first on the list:

- Prepare carefully, don't just avoid it by ignoring it. It may not be 'alright on the night'.
- Think about what you might be asked. Ask you tutors what format will be followed, how long it will last and what topics might come up.
- Make a list of the questions you might have to answer and particularly prepare the topics you know are your weak points. There is nowhere to hide in a viva, you cannot ignore the question and there is *nothing* quite as soul destroying as having to say 'I don't know' several times early on in the interview.
- Practice giving spoken answers. You will most likely be unfamiliar with answering direct questions, so get a fellow student, friend or relative to ask you questions. The more you practise the better and more polished your answers will become.
- When you're in the room:
  - Don't waffle, or invent answers. Be honest and if you don't know, say so.
  - Listen carefully to the questions. Like reading the questions in a written paper, your nerves might get in the way and you may become prone to mis-hearing the question. Check if necessary.
  - Don't get arrogant, defensive or offensive. It will only get up the examiner's nose.

Model Answer 6: *Plan for Workshop on Personal Support*

Aims:

To examine different types of support in our lives, beyond professional supervision.
To look critically at our support networks and ask if they are sufficient.

Outline of what the session will cover:

1. Examine your present support system.
2. Is it enough?
    What kind of support is positive?
    What kind of support is missing?
3. What kind of support do you want?
4. What stops or blocks you from getting it?
5. What can you do about some or all of these blocks?

Materials:

Flip chart, pens and paper; handout; question sheet on personal support.

Timetable, content and methods:

2pm

Introduce workshop. Talk about personal support systems and how this is wider than just supervision - is supervision enough? Brainstorm 'What support means to me'. Write answers on flipchart looking out for and acknowledging any gender or cultural differences.

2.15pm

Divide into small groups, give flipchart paper & pens to each group, ask them to draw 'personal support map'.

2.30pm

Feedback from groups - spokesperson from each group.

2.50pm

Give handout on different types of support then break for 10 minutes. Ask participants to read them during break!

3.00pm

Give out question sheet on 'Blocks to support'. Split into talker and listener pairs to facilitate exploration of questions.

3.40pm

Feedback on pairs work, discussion.

3.50pm

Concluding comments on personal support and feedback on workshop. Hand out workshop evaluation sheets for collection by tutors afterwards.

Tutor's comments

This is a good plan for a workshop. Your aims are clear - although it might have been a good idea to relate it more to being a trainee counsellor. You have included a variety of activities and you are clear about the timing of each segment. The handouts were clear and not too wordy. A bibliography would have been an improvement.

On the day you discovered that this was too ambitious i.e. you put too much into the time allowed. I actually think that the plan itself is properly proportioned in terms of time. What happened on the day was that although your presentation of the material and exercises (which I thought were great) was good, you lost your grip on the timing. Learning how to stop discussions is a skill worth having! As you saw from the feedback sheets, everyone thought it was a good pass. Me too! Well done.

Hints and Tips 7

1. **Client tapes:**
   • Take care to select a suitable client and a suitable tape. Show off your skills, don't pick one that you think will only just scrape through.
   • Get good equipment and accommodation.
   • Check the equipment before you use it.
   • Make sure you have the fully informed consent of your client. Make sure you are following all the appropriate ethical guidelines.

2. **Presentations, seminars and workshops:**
   • Make a plan and stick to it.
   • Vary the activities to hold the audiences attention.
   • Allow plenty of time - you're almost bound to try to fit too much in.
   Prepare your handouts, OHP transparencies well in advance.
   • Have a practice or run-through with a friend or relative as a critical audience. Time yourself.
   • On the day itself - relax. Introduce yourself. If you're extremely nervous it sometimes helps to say so.
   • Have a good ending to round it off. Don't just 'stop'.

3. **Case study or presentation:**
   • In addition to the points above, make sure you have photocopied enough materials to go round - you may be surprised by some last minute additions to the audience.
   • Be sure to make appropriate arrangements for the collection and disposal of confidential material.

4. **Viva or oral exam**
   • In the unlikely event that you will have to face a viva, do prepare for it. It won't go away if you ignore it. Relax.
   • Listen carefully to the questions you are asked, get clarification if you are not sure.
   • Don't waffle.
   • Every minute you spend listening is a minute you're not talking.

New Technology and Learning Counselling

8

Since the first edition of this book, developments in technology have continued to have an impact upon the world in general and an increasing impact upon the world of counselling. As a trainee in counselling you may be encouraged to use word processing software on personal computers to enhance the presentation of your assignments. Also, you may have seen the 'hype' surrounding the fabled 'information superhighway' and wondered what all the fuss is about. This chapter will attempt a beginners' guide to both of these technologies and, hopefully, demystify them enough for you to have a go.

The personal computer - don't switch off yet!
Even though the UK boasts one of the highest number of personal computers per family in the developed world, there are still millions of people who, either from personal choice or lack of opportunity, have never used one. I think it is fairly obvious that computers are here to stay and they are being increasingly incorporated into learning situations of all kinds. The whole computer revolution is based upon the idea that *they are easy to use*. If you are frightened of computers or keyboards it will do no harm to bear this in mind - always remember that nearly everyone has the *capacity* to use them, even though some readers will not have the *desire* to use them.

When it comes to making life easier for learners

(whether on a counselling course or whatever) computers have a definite contribution to make, so think carefully before dismissing them as being only of interest to computer freaks or games addicts.

The factors that make computer-mediated communication different from other forms of communication are:
• Speed
  Computers send and receive information very quickly. If you had to exchange the same information by post or by going to the library or by buying books it would take you days or even weeks instead of minutes or hours.
• Convenience
  If you have a computer at home, you don't have to go anywhere, you simply sit down in front of the keyboard and start sending messages ('letters' to your friends, requests for information or answers to other people's queries for example). This ease of access is very useful for people with mobility difficulties, whether due to physical disability, childcare responsibilities or whatever.
• Range of information
  Your local (even large city) library simply cannot compete with the fantastic range of information that a computer can access if it is fitted with a modem and suitable software. It is possible to access whole 'libraries' (sometimes literally a real library) of information from leisure interests to

highly technical subjects without leaving your home, and many of these 'libraries' are free.

Access to personal computers

The first stage in becoming computer literate is to get hold of a personal computer. By 'get hold of' I do not necessarily mean that you should go out and buy one. There are opportunities to use personal computers without spending £500 or so, for example:

• family and friends

Friends and relatives may be happy for you to use their computer for word processing and internet access. You may need to work out how to pay them for internet access but this should not be difficult between friends.

• your college or training institute

Colleges usually have resource centres or sections of the library where PCs are available for the completion of assignments and some will have internet access. (You may have to pay extra for this.)

• your local library

Some libraries provide access to PCs - ask where the nearest facility is for you. Again, you may have to pay extra for this facility.

• a local technology centre

Primarily open for local business to use, you might be able to use the facilities (which usually include fax and photocopying) for a fee. Some rural towns and villages have technology centres for residents' use.

• an 'Internet Cafe'

These are regular cafes where you can buy a coffee and sandwich but in addition to tables and chairs they provide desks with PCs linked up to the Internet. It will cost around £5 - £10 per hour

to use the machines. This is an expensive way to access the Internet.

What may have escaped your attention is that nearly all of these methods of getting access to the Internet will also put you in touch with people. Far from isolating you from others, using technology in this way is just as likely to introduce you to more people and give you something to talk about.

Your personal computer

If you already have a personal computer and wish to access the Internet, you will need to make sure that its technical specifications are good enough to do the job. Similarly, if you are contemplating buying a PC, you will need one that has the capability to connect you to the Internet.

The rough rule-of -thumb is to buy the fastest, 'biggest' computer you can afford.
• Fast means that its processor runs at a high speed.
• Big means that it has lots of memory (RAM) inside and it has a large hard disk (nowadays measured in gigabytes).

Since computer specifications change daily, making predictions is silly. The best advice is to find a friend or relative to give you some information or buy a computer magazine or look in 'Which?' magazine in your local library or go to a large computer shop or warehouse and ask for advice. Obviously these sources have different degrees of impartiality when it comes to recommending machines, but don't be put off. You will not have to become a computer expert in order to buy a computer, but you will need to learn a little about the machines in order to get the best out of one.

The Internet and 'information superhighway'

First it will help to explain some terms. As with everything else relating to computers, this is easy to understand, so don't give up.

Firstly, your Server

A modem and telephone line will not automatically get you access to the Internet. You will have to purchase a service (a sort of gateway to the 'Net) from a *server*. You will probably have seen adverts for servers in magazines and newspapers or you may even have had trial discs and junk mail from Internet service providers. The cost of Internet access plus e-mail is coming down all of the time, but at the time of writing you can get Internet access and e-mail for a small monthly charge depending upon the length of time you sign up for and the level of service you require. The best way of finding out about service providers and what they offer is to ask a friend, relative or work colleague to give you their recommendations. You could also buy a magazine dedicated to the Internet and check through the various adverts, or look in 'Which?'

The Internet

If a computer has a modem, you can get access to the Internet. A modem is simply a box of electronics which enables the computer to send and receive messages down a standard telephone line. The computer will be connected to the telephone line and it can then dial up and communicate with other computers. This, in simple terms is the basis of the Internet. (You may need to get a second phone line if either you or a member of your family start using the Internet a lot.) The Internet is an international network of computers made possible by computer programmes which allow the computers to 'talk' to each other, i.e., exchange information. This international network is most useful in two ways, firstly it enables you to send and receive electronic mail or e-mail. Second it allows you to have access to the World Wide Web. In other words, the Internet is a communications arena, a series of possible connections between computers all over the world.

The World Wide Web

Once you have access to the Internet via a modem and appropriate software, you can connect to any computer in the World Wide Web. Computers all over the world provide information for others to access (mostly free, but sometimes there's a charge) on what is known as *Web Pages* or *Web Sites*. A reasonable analogy is to think of the Web as a High Street or market. There are all kinds of shop fronts for you yo look in, some providing goods for sale, some commercial services, some educational institutions like universities, some are libraries, some are charities and some are individuals who buy a space to set up their stall like a car boot sale. As a counselling trainee you are most likely to be interested in official libraries, but you would be well advised to look in the car boot section for a couple of reasons, firstly, there are some very dedicated individuals (see the panel on page 156) who pour hours of effort into creating a website featuring a special interest they might have. There are some counsellors who are brilliant at this. Secondly, remember, the internet is open to anyone for very little - or sometimes no - cost, and it may be that a counsellor is emigrating to Australia to start a new career as a computer consultant and wants to sell all of their books.

The trouble with the Web is that it is just so big. It is so big by virtue of all of the car boot type people who buy a space for a few pounds and set out their stall as a shrine to pay homage to Kylie Minogue or an opportunity to show people their holiday snaps. It is so big that it defies a person's attempts to search through it without the assistance of a *search engine* or *web crawler*. These are computer services which run directories of web sites and search through the millions of sites (stalls and shops) to find any that are offering the information you require. There is more detail on how to get counselling information from the Web on page 156. Without an engine or crawler it's next to impossible to find the web pages with particular information on and even then it is a process with a high degree of uncertainty. If you simply type a name into an engine, such as 'Carl Rogers', you are just as likely to find a 'Carl Rogers' web page which declares:

Hi! I'm Carl Rogers, sheep farmer in Queensland, Australia. My interests are sheep shearing and keeping an archive on Neighbours. This shrine dedicated to Kylie Minogue....

Each Web Site has its own unique address called a URL (uniform resource locator) - a series of letters and symbols such as:

http://www.eap-info.co.uk/   (try it)

which functions just like a postcode. It enables people searching the net to find the page in question from the many millions available, so if you know the URL of the site that holds the information you require you don't need to go searching. Furthermore, most web site owners have realised how frustrating it can be to search the web with an engine, so they include what are known as *links* on their page which will take you quickly and easily to pages with similar subjects and information.

E-mail

Electronic mail is now available to everyone who has a computer. It works like this; you have an e-mail address unique to you. You also have a 'mailbox' located in the server's computer to which anyone knowing your address can send mail. You can send mail to anyone whose e-mail address you know. You simply look in your mailbox to retrieve mail sent to you.

E-mail may be useful to counselling trainees in a few ways:

• You may be able to contact tutors, librarians or administrators in your College or training organisation using e-mail to book tutorials, renew bookloans etc.

E-mail jargon

Flaming: Insulting someone or using foul language.
Spamming: Sending junk mail or unasked for adverts.
Snail mail: regular mail delivered to your door.

Indicate your feelings in an e-mail message by using the following punctuation symbols:

:-)	Happy
:-(	Sad
;-)	Wink (Joke)

• You may be able to keep in touch with fellow trainees out of course times, to swap information on assignments or good books etc.

• You may be able to join counselling-dedicated discussion groups, giving you access to often lively, topical exchanges of mail on counselling-related subjects between people all over the world.

E-mail may sound rather dull and you may wonder what use it could be when you can easily phone up your friends or write to them. Until you have tried it, it's difficult to explain quite how much impact the apparently limited advantages of e-mail can have on personal and business (or training-related) communications. Some of the advantages of e-mail are:

• you can send mail at any time of day (taking advantage of cheap rate calls if you wish) and it will arrive at its destination address within minutes.

• The addressee will pick up their mail whenever it's convenient and the mail will simply wait in the mailbox until its picked up. This means that you can send mail without worrying whether the addressee is at home. The addressee can reply as soon as they choose. This can be a matter of minutes or hours, and usually it's the same day.

• You can send mail to the opposite side of the world without worrying about time zones. The addressee will simply pick up the mail and respond during their normal working or social time.

• You can carefully consider whatever you wish to say rather than get stuck for words.

• Business or social transactions can be completed much more quickly than by mail, and documents (such as contracts or journal papers) can be sent attached to e-mails, then printed out by the receiving computer.

I was surprised by how quickly I became an e-mail fan, corresponding with professional colleagues, friends and even relatives. From simple things like arranging a family gathering with my brother (we can both be difficult to get hold of on the phone sometimes) through discussing assignments with an external examiner, to arranging a mortgage with a financial adviser are all activities wholly or partly completed by e-mail by me in the past year.

Glossary

Browser: The software that provides the viewing window to the net on your computer and enables you to move between sites. Common ones are Netscape Communicator and Internet Explorer. They are always being updated to enable users to get more things more quickly from the net.

Chat rooms: these are interactive websites where you can type in messages in real time online, as opposed to the delay in e-mail.

Offline: writing and reading messages when not connected to the net via your phoneline. It saves on phone bills.

Bookmarks: store the addresses of your favourite sites so that you can locate them quickly without typing in lots of letters and symbols.

How to locate good counselling sites . . . . . .

Essentially there are three ways to 'surf', 'navigate' 'explore' or 'browse' the World Wide Web. Which one you choose depends upon how much you know about the Web, whether you know the site you are trying to get to, how much time you've got and finally whether anyone else has set up a series of helpful signposts to assist fellow navigators.

1. Using a search engine
I'm starting off with the worst, most frustrating, time-consuming way to find anything on the Web, yet few people ever get beyond this method. It is also what we all do when all else fails.

When you get on to the home page of your server you will have an option to click on 'search' or 'world wide web' or something similar. After clicking on this you may be presented with a choice of named search engines, such as 'Yahoo', 'AltaVista' and 'Lycos'. If not you will probably be only given the option of your server's own proprietary engine (usually these are not anywhere as good as the others). There will be a box marked 'search' inviting you to type in a word or phrase and a 'go' or 'find' button to activate the search process.
• Do not type in *counselling* and hit the 'find' button. In the first place you will get all sites that have anything to do with counselling (including 57 varieties of financial and business counselling). Sorting through this lot would be impossible. In the second place, you have forgotten that most sites will be American (US) and use the American spelling *counseling*.

• Do find out the correct grammar to use in your 'search' dialogue box. All systems have help pages to assist you in this. It is essential to target your search more closely, such as using hyphens to link words or inverted commas or even capital letters to create inclusive categories or indicate proper names.
• The very first thing to do when you hit on a website that has useful information or links in it is to bookmark it. That way you will be able to return to it almost instantly without going through the tedious process of searching all over again.
• The next thing you should do when you find a site that looks any good, is to start using the 'links' to navigate your way around the topic. Links are connections between Web Sites that share a topic in common, so you will have a good idea that you will be chasing your chosen subject. Links are clearly marked on Web pages as 'Links'.

2. Using a library or magazine
Another, sometimes more useful feature of some search engines, is the facility whereby they provide libraries of Web Sites. These are usually held in categories such as 'Health', 'News' and 'Entertainment'. The idea is to search through a branching system of sub-categories until you get to the one(s) you want, as follows:
• I started on AltaVista (which I think is particularly good at this - you can choose 'Zones' and 'Libraries'.
• Click on 'Health Library'.
• Click on 'Browse Categories'.
• From the choice presented I clicked on 'Health and Fitness'.
• Then I chose 'Conditions/Illnesses'.

on the Web

• From the next list I chose 'Mental Health'.
• From this list I clicked on 'Counseling and Therapy'.
• Bingo! I was up for a laugh so I tried 'Other Therapies' from this list and got...well I'll let you try for yourself.

I find this a better way to get information on a specific topic than using the 'search' facility. I seem to find many more official sites this way and get loads of junk sites, especially ones offering 'adult' material, when using 'search'.

Going direct to favourite sites

This is by far the best method of locating counselling related information on the web. You can collect good URLs along the way as you search or surf and store them as bookmarks, but it can take time. Here is a short list of good sites and their URLs that are correct at the time of going to press. It is important to know that the location of some sites can change. If you use the net regularly for information retrieval this may not be too much of a problem, but updating your bookmarks can be a bit of a fag. Some Servers provide browsers that are capable of doing this automatically.

I have hardly sorted these sites at all because sites are constantly being developed. Nevertheless I recommend you start with a site with lots of links such as Allan Turner's homepage or Counseling Resources on the Net. I have not given lots of details of what they provide since this will change on a monthly basis. Some will have disappeared by the time you read this, and new ones will have appeared. Finally, I want to pay tribute to Allan Turner for the huge amount of

work put into his site. It is the place I go first to find out what's happening in Person-Centred Counselling on the Net. In fact it's a good starting point for anyone since he has links to many other non-PC counselling and therapy sites too. Visit his site now!

Counselling Websites

Allan Turner http://users.powernet.co.uk/
PC bias, great links, news, events, students, generally fab.
BAC http://www.counselling.co.uk/
sections on accreditation, membership, publications, accredited courses, find-a-therapist, etc.
Counseling Resources on the Net
http://www.csun.edu/~hfedp001/links.html
mainly US links, but good never-the-less.
Assoc for the Development of the Person-Centred Approach (ADPCA) http://www.adpca.org/
events, membership, free PC papers to download, etc.
Center for Studies of the Person
http://www.centerfortheperson.org/
best site for PC resources, e.g. videos of Carl Rogers, etc.
American Counseling Assoc
http://www.counseling.org/
US links, publications & events, schools/college bias.
American Psychological Assoc http://www.apa.org/
the best US site. Worth a visit, good library & resources.
The Gestalt Therapy page http://www.getsalt.org/
good UK links, find-a-therapist, events etc.

Some of these sites have free essays, papers and extracts from books to download. The best opportunities are on Allan Turner's page, the ADPCA page and the American Psychological Association page. Happy surfing!

Hints and Tips 8

Pros and Cons of New Technology for Counselling

Starting with the Cons
- It costs money to use of own a computer.
- Computers can cause illnesses: Techno-phobia, Ludite-itis, tennis elbow and stiff neck.
- They can also make Computer widows widowers/orphans.

The Pros are easy
Computers do three main things for you.
1. They will help with all **written assignments** that you have to do.
   - They keep notes, ideas, plans and references that can with ease be turned into essays without you having to write the words twice.
   - They will produce a piece that will not get the comment 'I can't read your writing.'
   - Tutors prefer to read type.
   - *They make your life easier!*

2. They give you access to the vast world (literally) of counselling.
   - You have access to all the counselling and psychotherapy classics as well as being able to partake in new ideas that are just forming.
   - If you are serious about counselling you need to know how to access the **Internet**.

3. Instead of isolating us from others, as is a popular misconception, computers actually put us in touch with real people all over the world within minutes via e-mail.

You will need:
- The courage to jump in and learn an new skill if you are not familiar with this 'new' technology.
- The biggest, fastest computer you can afford.
- A modem.
- A telephone line (or as second one if the one you already have is well used).
- Internet access, via server software.
- The list of World Wide Web addresses on p.157.
- An e-mail address of your own.
- Time to play and learn.

References

Anderson, D.R., Alwitt, L.F., Lorsch, E.P. and Levin, F.R. (1979) Watching Children Watch Television in G. Hale and M.Lewis (eds) *Attention and the Development of Cognitive Skills* Plenum: New York.

Bell, J. (1993) *Doing Your Research Project 2nd Edition* Open University Press.

Bruner, J.S. and Minturn, A.L. (1955) Perceptual identification and perceptual organisation. *Journal of General Psychology* 53, 21-8.

Inskipp, F. and Proctor, B. (1993) *The Art, Craft and Tasks of Counselling Supervision. Part 1: Making the Most of Supervision.* Cascade Publications. (Available from Cascade Publications, 4 Ducks Walk, Twickenham, Middlesex.)

Harlow, H.F. (1949) The formation of learning sets. *Psychological Review* 56, 52-65.

Heron, J. (1988) Assessment Revisited, in Boud, D. *Developing Student Autonomy in Learning,* London: Kogan Page.

Kolb, D.A. (1984) *Experiential Learning.* Englewood Cliffs, NJ: Prentice -Hall.

Lewin, Kurt (1951) *Field Theory in Social Science* New York: Harper.

Mearns, D. (1993) in W Dryden (Ed) *Questions and Answers on Counselling in Action.* London: Sage.

Purton, C. (1991) Selection and Assessment in Counsellor Training Courses **in** Dryden, W. and Thorne, B. (Eds) *Training and Supervision for Counselling in Action.* London: Sage.

Rogers, C.R. (1951) *Client-Centred Therapy.* London: Constable.

Rogers, C.R. (1961) *On Becoming a Person.* London: Constable.

Sanders, P. and Liptrot, D. (1993) *An Incomplete Guide to Basic Research Methods and Data Collection For Counsellors.* Manchester: PCCS.

Sanders, P. and Liptrot, D. (1994) *An Incomplete Guide to Qualitative Research Methods for Counsellors.* Manchester: PCCS.

Tudor, K. (1997) Book Reviews. *Person-Centred Practice,* Volume 5, No.1. 33-4

Addresses

The British Association for Counselling
1 Regent Place, Rugby, Warwickshire, CV21 2PJ.
Information Line 01788 578328
Office 01788 550899
Fax 01788 562189

British Association for the Person-Centred Approach
BM BAPCA
London
WC1N 3XX

Independent Practitioners' Network
c/o Nick Totton
326 Burley Rd
Leeds
LS4 2NZ

Person-Centred Approach
& Client-Centred Therapy
Essential Readers
Series editor Tony Merry

Person-Centred Therapy
A Revolutionary Paradigm

Jerold Bozarth

Jerold D. Bozarth is Professor Emeritus of the University of Georgia. In this book he presents a collection of revised papers and new writings on Person-Centred therapy representing over 40 years' work as an innovator and theoretician. This book is essential reading for all with an interest in Client-Centred Therapy and the Person-Centred Approach.

• • •

SACRED SCIENCE
Person-centred Inquiry into the Spiritual and the Subtle

John Heron

Heron writes: *'This book is about my own lived inquiry in the spiritual and subtle field, about a radical revision of ...onal theory, and about a pioneer form of sacred science in which human beings co-operate together to inquire in ...s manner into their own spiritual and subtle experience, without prior allegiance to any existing school.'*

• • •

IMPLAUSIBLE PROFESSIONS
Arguments for Pluralism and Autonomy in Psychotherapy and Counselling

edited by Richard House and Nick Totton

...counselling and psychotherapy that demands to be read. A book that wasn't commissioned by Sage, isn't ...ne trainers for captive students, but one that is compelling, uncomfortable, uneven, likely to be unpopular ...and is unequivocally passionate committed and honest...What you get here is a lot of what Virginia Satir ...ng' - telling the honest truth. . .Together they [the authors] demonstrate the persistence in many ...oners of a deep tenacity and groundedness that resist the creeping 'McDonaldisation' of the treatment ...e that the professionalisation process has ushered in.'David Kalisch *Self & Society March 1998*

• • •

you sitting uncomfortably? Windy Dryden Live and Uncut

Windy Dryden

...challenging lectures deliverd by Britain's most widely published counsellor. Readers will probably ...den as author and editor of over 100 books on counselling and psychotherapy. Now read him at his ...censored in these stimulating lectures. Be prepared to be stirred by his outspoken attempts both to ...world of counselling. Trainers, trainees and practitioners should be ready to respond to his

---

Index

Index

Person-Centred Therapy
A Revolutionary Paradigm

Jerold Bozarth

Jerold D. Bozarth is Professor Emeritus of the University of Georgia. In this book he presents a collection of revised papers and new writings on Person-Centred therapy representing over 40 years' work as an innovator and theoretician. This book is essential reading for all with an interest in Client-Centred Therapy and the Person-Centred Approach.

• • •

SACRED SCIENCE
Person-centred Inquiry into the Spiritual and the Subtle

John Heron

John Heron writes: *'This book is about my own lived inquiry in the spiritual and subtle field, about a radical revision of transpersonal theory, and about a pioneer form of sacred science in which human beings co-operate together to inquire in a rigorous manner into their own spiritual and subtle experience, without prior allegiance to any existing school.'*

• • •

IMPLAUSIBLE PROFESSIONS
Arguments for Pluralism and Autonomy in Psychotherapy and Counselling
edited by Richard House and Nick Totton

'At last a book on counselling and psychotherapy that demands to be read. A book that wasn't commissioned by Sage, isn't written by big name trainers for captive students, but one that is compelling, uncomfortable, uneven, likely to be unpopular in some quarters, and is unequivocally passionate committed and honest...What you get here is a lot of what Virginia Satir once called 'levelling' - telling the honest truth...Together they [the authors] demonstrate the persistence in many humanistic practitioners of a deep tenacity and groundedness that resist the creeping 'McDonaldisation' of the treatment of contemporary woe that the professionalisation process has ushered in.'David Kalisch *Self & Society March 1998*

• • •

Are you sitting uncomfortably? Windy Dryden Live and Uncut
Windy Dryden

12 thought-provoking and challenging lectures deliverd by Britain's most widely published counsellor. Readers will probably be familiar with Windy Dryden as author and editor of over 100 books on counselling and psychotherapy. Now read him at his irrepressible best; live and uncensored in these stimulating lectures. Be prepared to be stirred by his outspoken attempts both to provoke and illuminate the world of counselling. Trainers, trainees and practitioners should be ready to respond to his discomforting challenges.